LIFE OF MICHAEL

Jeremy Novick is a well-known journalist and author. He has previously written an authorised biography of Morecambe and Wise, and a biography of Tommy Cooper, as well as two books on football. A former television critic for the *Independent*, he is currently the TV and music critic of the *Express*. He lives in Brighton, so travels a lot.

LIFE OF MICHAEL

An Illustrated Biography
of Michael Palin

Jeremy Novick

TED SMART

For Gilly, juicy and lovely. And . . . as ever, to Elly and LouLou, Maxwell Wolf, Lexa and Rose – perfectly formed, everything a boy could wish for.

To Michael Palin who said 'Yes' and took time out from planning his assault on the Sahara. It was extraordinarily kind and generous and, listen, you know all that stuff about him being a nice bloke . . . he is. Thanks to Roger Mills, Terry Jones, Robert Hewison and everyone else who talked to me. Ella and Anoushka and . . . Thanks to Tinu, Alex and Nigel at the *Express*, Mal, John, Fiona and Sharon at Essential, and Sacha and Martin at home.

And lastly, to my mum and dad, who in their own ways are always there.

First published in 2001
by HEADLINE BOOK PUBLISHING

This edition produced for The Book People Ltd, Hall Wood Avenue, Haydock, St Helens, WA11 9UL

© ESSENTIAL BOOKS LTD 2001

The right of Jeremy Novick to be identified as the Author of this Work has been asserted by him in accordance with the Copyright, Designs and Patents Act 1988.

10 9 8 7 6 5 4 3 2 1

A CIP catalogue record for this book is available from the British Library

ISBN 0-7472-3529-5

HEADLINE BOOK PUBLISHING
A division of Hodder Headline
338 Euston Road
London NW1 3BH

www.headline.co.uk
www.hodderheadline.com

PHOTOGRAPHIC CREDITS
page 49 © Alpha; page 65 © Alpha/D Benett, page 140 © Alpha/Richard Chambery; page 19 © Alpha/Robin Price; pages 113, 126, 128, 137, 143 © BBC/Basil Pau; pages 88, 91, 101 © BBC; pages 118, 125 © Channel 4; pages 70, 87 © Drew Mara; page 147 © Katz Pictures/Harry Borden; page 154 Katz Pictures/Cable Guide; page 8 © Katz Pictures/Chris Saunders; pages 74, 77, 82 (bottom), 93 (bottom), 94-5, 97, 98, 100 © The Kobal Collection; pages 7, 96 © The Kobal Collection/David Farrell; page 103 © The Kobal Collection/David James; page 60 © The Kobal Collection/Drew Mara; page 33 (top right, top left) © Mander & Mitchenson; pages 34, 36, 38-9 © Pearson TV; pages 10, 14, 33 (bottom), 40, 42, 68, 73, 76, 81, 82 (top), 93 (top), 122 © Pictorial Press; page 105 © Pictorial Press/David Appleby; pages 54, 59 © Python Pictures Ltd; pages 23, 24, 148 © Rex Features; page 32 © Rex Features/Azadour Guzelian; page 46 © Rex Features/Tony Kyriacou; page 151 © Rex Features/Ralph Metzger; pages 2, 26, 108, 132, 144 © Scope Features; pages 50, 52-3, 55, 71 © Terry Gilliam.

The author and publishers have made every reasonable effort to contact all copyright holders. Any errors that may have occurred are inadvertent and anyone who for any reason has not been contacted is invited to write to the publishers so that a full acknowledgement may be made in subsequent editions of this work.

Printed and bound in Spain by Bookprint, S.L., Barcelona
Reproduction by P2 Digital

Contents

Prologue 6

Chapter One   A Lovely Man Doing a Lovely Job, Living a Lovely Life 9

Chapter Two   Alone Together 27

Chapter Three   The Gathering 35

Chapter Four   'It's . . . ' 47

Chapter Five   Creative Tensions and Marital Fatigue 61

Chapter Six   The Post-*Python* Landscape 89

Chapter Seven   The Passport Years 109

Chapter Eight   The Last of the Big Journeys 133

Chapter Nine   The Dark Side of Michael Palin 145

Chapter Ten   The Last of the Big Journeys – Part 2 149

Epilogue 155

Index 159

Prologue

This is a true story. A while ago, we had our neighbours round for drinks and a bite to eat. We knew them as neighbours but we didn't know them particularly well and they seemed nice, nice enough to want to get to know better. Anyway, I was talking to the woman and she told me how she was a solicitor now, but had been an actress.

'Really?' I said. 'What have you been in? Anything I'd know?'

'It was a while ago now, but I was in *Monty Python's Meaning of Life* and a film called *The Missionary*. I only had small parts . . .'

My ears pricked up. This was perfect. I was, I explained, thinking of writing a book about Michael Palin.

'Do you remember him well?' I asked. 'What was he like?'

She looked at me and smiled. 'I do remember. He was really nice. A lovely man. I remember one day on set he asked me into his trailer for a coffee . . .' It's sad to say, but what little journalist there is in me leaped with the hope of a bit of gossip. 'And he really took time out to talk to me about my career and where it was going. He was really helpful. A lovely man.'

In The Missionary *(1983)*

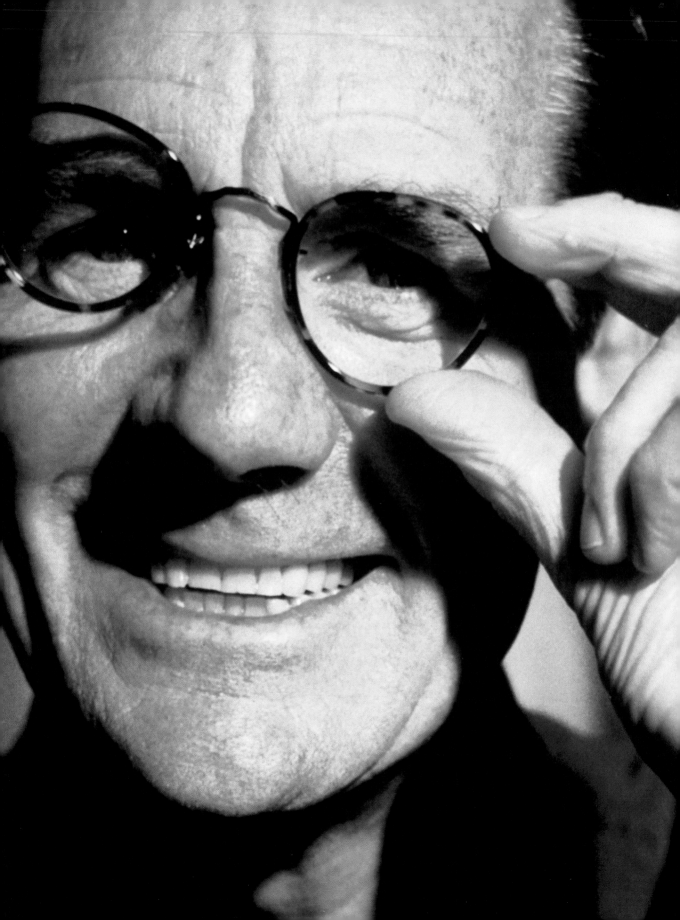

Chapter One

A Lovely Man Doing a Lovely Job, Living a Lovely Life

'John, Michael, Eric, the Terrys and the handsome one who died, they were all such lovely men. Especially Michael.'

HAZEL PETHIG, COSTUME DESIGNER ON THE PYTHON SHOWS

Michael Palin. That nice Michael Palin. For the last thirty years, that nice Michael Palin has been the most consistently popular person in the world of television entertainment. He was a prime mover in the most innovative British television programme of the last thirty years, he's starred in films that have made Hollywood sit up and take notice, and has acted alongside the likes of Maggie Smith, Denholm Elliott and Robert De Niro (who got the role Palin didn't want). He's written books, plays, children's stories, dramas, film screenplays and a novel, he's made records and radio programmes. And in the process of doing all this, he's achieved just about everything we all desire: creative fulfilment, financial riches, domestic bliss, personal happiness. He's good-looking, fit and healthy. He's not fat and he hasn't lost his hair. He's got a lovely wife and three children whom he loves and who love him. He's stayed true to himself, hasn't got lost in ego. He still lives where he's always lived, sent his kids to the local state school and campaigns for the environment. By any yardstick, he's been fantastically successful in whatever he turns his hand to. He's universally liked by his public and his peers and no one has anything remotely resembling a bad word to say about him.

Shall we go home now?

Monty Python's Flying Circus first started in 1969 – over thirty years ago – and Palin is the same genial bloke now that he was then. He looks more or less the same as he always has, carries the same air of affable amiability, the same smile. Yet for all his non-threatening presence and clean-cut acceptability, he is more subversive now than he was back in the good old days when he was a satirical comic writing barbs for David Frost or taking the piss out of rigid societal structures with the Pythons, because, like all the best subversives, he drives his own bus. He plays his game according to his rules and according to his morality. You never see him anywhere except on his own programmes, the programmes that he wants to make that are made by people he trusts. You don't see him in adverts; you don't see him on comedy panel shows; you don't see him on chat shows unless he's got a new show to promote, and then, if not exactly under sufferance, it's done through a sense of duty, a sense of it being part of the 'work'.

Palin's personal popularity bears no relation to media profiles and the rise of the vacuous celebrity. In an age when people are famous for being famous, figures like Michael Palin are thin on the ground. That he turned his back on the big-time Hollywood stardom that was surely beckoning after the success of *A Fish Called Wanda* and returned to embrace the small screen in his own country is striking in itself. Forget all the writing and stuff for a minute. He's a good enough actor in his

The early days (from left): Terry Jones, Graham Chapman, John Cleese, Eric Idle, Terry Gilliam and Michael Palin

own right to have made that cross-Atlantic breakthrough, but it simply didn't appeal, and why do something that you don't want to do?

Maybe one explanation for Palin's success is that we like to think he operates in an old-fashioned world, a world where people are nice and friendly, smiley and honest. People don't look at Palin and think 'OK, so he might be ridiculously talented, but I'm a nice person. I've stayed true to myself. I might not have scaled those particular heights, but listen, I haven't sold out. I haven't drowned any kittens or broken any eggs . . . '

When his last series, *Michael Palin's Hemingway's Adventure,* started, I, like all good television journalists, interviewed Michael and wrote the standard 'He's a nice bloke' piece. While waiting to see him, I talked to the programme producer. 'What's his secret?' I asked. I wasn't looking for any gossip or any of that other newspaper stuff. I was just curious. 'There's no secret,' he said. 'He's just a lovely man doing a lovely job, living a lovely life.'

'"A lovely man doing a lovely job, living a lovely life." Did he really say that?' said Michael when I put it to him. 'That's very nice, but . . . well, I like to think I'm not the only one doing that. I like to think that most people on the production were the same.'

'I don't envy you your job,' said Roger Mills, Palin's producer on *Around the World in Eighty Days, Pole to Pole* and *Full Circle,* 'because in a sense he's as near-perfect a person as you can find and that doesn't necessarily make terribly exciting reading.'

But the Babies Needed Strangling

It may be best to get it out of the way early on. Michael Palin, are you the nicest man in the world?

'I can't believe you've asked me that. I can't believe you've asked me that. I'm going to get a Japanese battle sword out and slice you in two.' Maybe I was being unreasonable. Maybe I did deserve it. But people will still say, 'Ah well, he did it with a smile on his face. He was a baby strangler but, you know, the babies needed strangling.'

That nice Michael Palin. It's like the joke about how people thought their football team was called Tottenham Hotspur Nil. The 'n' word has almost become part of Palin's name. After thirty years at the top of the tree, after thirty-five years in which he's touched almost every branch of the entertainment business, more often than not with success, the thing that Palin has become known for is being nice and although the word 'nice' denotes good things, it's not actually a nice word. 'Nice' means anodyne, harmless, characterless. When he answered that question, it was the only occasion during my time with Palin that he looked remotely angry. Well, animated.

Does it annoy him?

> It doesn't really worry me and I try not to get too drawn into it. I was talking to someone in an interview and they brought that up, and I said, 'Of course I'm not the nicest person in the world,' and they said, 'Well, tell me some things you do that aren't nice,' and I thought, well, what sort of question is that? What do they want me to say? OK, I beat my wife – I don't actually, but I thought if you're going to get into that . . . this is ridiculous. I'm just going to have to live with it as a sort of cliché. Between you and me, it's quite a good defence against people prying too deeply. If that's what people want to say – Michael Palin: nicest man in the world – then they can put it out there. I think it must irritate people no end, which is probably why every now and then I do get some extremely abusive reviews – ferocious – and I think there must be a lot of people saying, 'God, that nice man again. I hate him. Why does everyone go on about him being nice?' That is a bit of a problem, but on the other hand I know I'm a complex person, but I don't want to explain it.

The best bit in that whole spiel is that 'I don't actually'. It tells you all you ever need to know about Michael. Maybe it's a double bluff, I don't know. Maybe he really is a wife beater . . . Most stars of his stature are, to a greater or lesser degree, egocentric, selfish monsters. That's as much a job description as a criticism. It could be that he's been famous – a star – for so long that he's passed through that egocentric stage, that he's seen it for what it is and has settled down, but Palin genuinely seems a nice bloke, a good chap . . . And it's difficult to find anyone to say any different.

John Cleese, for instance:

> Michael is immensely likeable and for me the best [Python] performer. I thought he had the biggest range and also he and I had a certain rapport as performers which was greater than I had with the others. Michael's great aim in life is to be affable, and this makes him enormously pleasant and enormously good company.

Terry Gilliam:

> Mike's gift when we were in the Pythons was his ease with dealing with things. Essentially, I think Mike was the one that everybody liked, he was the

one we could all agree on that we could like, because he was the easiest to work with.

Terry Jones:

I think Michael is a man of genius. He has a gift and the gift is life, in a way. It's how he touches the characters that he plays and that's where his best writing lay. What Mike's gift was to me was that he would come up with funny ideas that were magic. With most comic ideas, once the initial idea had been said, you could see the synthesis. You could see this and this and this and put it together and see how it's going to be funny. Mike would come up with things that . . . you couldn't see how you got there. Like the Spanish Inquisition. It's really, really funny, but there's no perceptible rationale behind it, or no perceptible comic analysis. To me, that's the most wonderful thing, when you can get comedy that is incapable of analysis and that's a kind of magical quality.

Carol Cleveland:

Eric always seemed a little distant, rather aloof. Terry Jones was very excitable, very fiery. Terry Gilliam was also very excitable but very visual and loud. Graham was a lovely man but did everything to excess. John was the most logical, definitely moody.

And as for Michael, well, Michael has never changed. He's the one that's never changed at all, and he remains the same charming, shy, sweet, helpful person that he is, and he is of course the only one who actually is quite shy and that's very appealing, which is why all the women adore Michael. He was always the ladies' favourite.

So he's nice. It's not a bad thing to be known as, and as a public image goes, it's not a bad suit to wear, as Palin himself acknowledges.

Well, no, it's not, but you've got to make sure that your suit isn't from Cliff Richard's or Gary Lineker's rack. That's the trouble – but there's nothing wrong with being nice to people. I also find that it's rather extraordinary that people should find it so unusual or worthy of note that I'm nice. I know a lot of people in this business who are nice. There are one or two shits around, but there are probably far fewer shits in this business than there are in some dreadful office, so it doesn't really hold up to examination anyway. If it's a

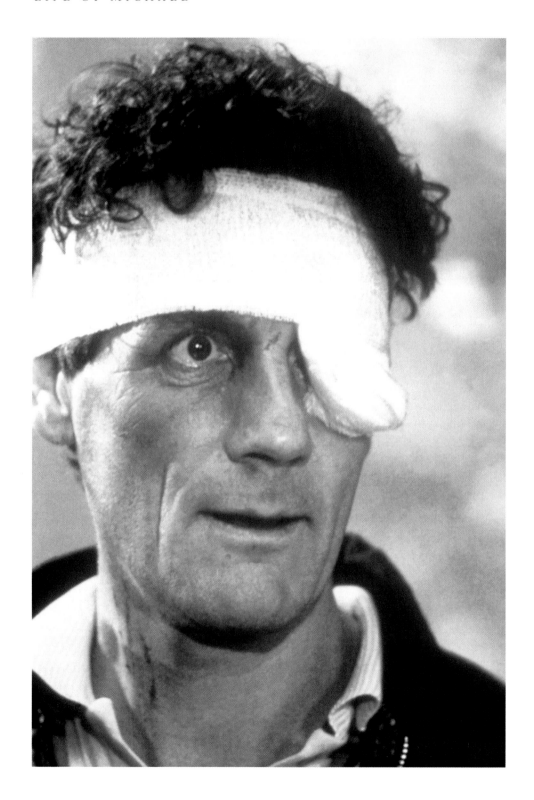

verdict on your programmes, meaning nice meaning harmless and inoffensive, then that worries me a little bit, but I've never seen it quite applied like that. They talk about my enthusiasm – my boyish enthusiasm – and I don't really mind that. That's fair enough. I have got enthusiasm. That's why I go into the programmes. If I was doing *Hamlet* and people talked about his boyish enthusiasm, I'd start to think. But in what I do, it's not a bad observation.

Occasionally people say things about you that you feel are spot on. I remember being interviewed by a journalist and they were all 'Tell us about your emotional life, tell us about your background, tell us about your sister's death,' and I'm happy to talk about almost anything that's happened in my life, but this was sort of everything about you in an hour and I've never done that with anyone. My wife, who I've been married to for thirty-two years, she came out in the end with the observation that I was someone who didn't like being scrutinized and I thought that was actually fair enough, quite a good use of the word. And I suppose I don't. I scrutinize myself. That's my job. I do that. That's what I want to do. The idea of someone in one hour revealing the real Michael Palin . . . It's so something that's so completely . . . unlikely.

Stories about Michael being anything other than decent are so few and far between that when one does turn up, it gets repeated and, in that Chinese whispers way, grows in venomous spleen – relatively speaking, of course. The most famous one concerns the time he was interviewed at home by a couple of young Oxford undergraduates, John Alachouzos and Edward Whitley, after Palin had made *The Missionary*. The interview was to be part of a book of interviews with famous people.

'Did you feel that *The Missionary* had the same quality of humour as *Life of Brian*?' asked Alachouzos.

'*Life of Brian* was a bit harder than *The Missionary*,' agreed Palin. He said that *The Missionary* was a more gentle film. '*Brian* was a series of sketches and observations about life now as well as life then. I don't think *The Missionary* had quite that aim.'

'Because,' continued Alachouzos, regardless, 'it struck me that the style of humour was out-of-date and rather slapstick.'

'I'm sorry you thought so,' said Palin.

'That scene when you explain to your wife what a fallen woman is,' said Alachouzos, 'and she asks if it is someone who has broken their ankle. How could you put that into the film?'

In A Fish Called Wanda *(1988)*

At which point . . .

'Oh dear,' said Palin. 'I'm sorry. It's just that I've got to go.' Palin made to go, but suddenly turned round. 'I mean, how can you ask a thing like that? What do you mean, how can I put it into the film? Because I happened to think it was funny. You didn't, fair enough. But don't come here and ask me how can I dare put something like that in a film? Honestly, that's the most pissing awful thing I've ever heard. If you didn't like the film, you didn't like the film, but don't say, "How can you put it in there?" . . .'

Again, Palin made to go, but again suddenly turned round. 'Because I'm an imbecile, because I'm no good at writing fucking comedy, that's why I put it in there.'

The best bit was yet to come. Palin stormed out of his own house, but then turned round and . . . 'Right, I'm off. Cheerio. I hope your thing comes out really well.'

It's a wonderful scene to imagine – though probably less wonderful to have participated in – and made a success of Alachouzos and Whitley's book. 'I'm not surprised that Michael got annoyed,' said Roger Mills:

> That's about the only thing you could say that would annoy him. He does get upset about being thought of as nice, but he is – and I think he wishes there was a bit more venom there . . . but there isn't. You almost feel like saying to him, 'Well, come on, Michael. Do something nasty.' He's as near-perfect to work with as you can get. I've worked with a lot of presenters – I've been doing this since 1961 and I've worked with a lot of people and I know how temperamental they are. Nearly always what you see on the screen is not the reality of that person, but in the case of Michael that is true. I mean, he is as nice off screen as he is on screen and that is actually very rare. He's a most incredibly organized person. He's doing several things at once on the travel programmes we do. He's doing the series and everything rests on him. Those series rise and fall not on what I do or what the camera crew does. If it's a success, it's Michael's success. If it fails, it's Michael's failure, so he knows he's carrying a huge responsibility. He's recognized almost everywhere we go. He is truly, truly international, so he has to field the adulation of tourists and local people. He has to pose for photos constantly. He's writing a book which has a pretty strict deadline, because the book has to coincide with the series. We travel with our own photographer, who has to have his pound of flesh as well. So he's writing the book, and he's writing a daily diary, he's talking his impressions into a dictaphone, he's doing the filming, he's meeting people all the time and he somehow manages to keep his good humour and sanity.
>
> Though as he gets older and as he gets more tired, there have been a couple of occasions when he has got ratty – I mean truly ratty – and then,

Michael being Michael, he's filled with remorse and apology. It's usually when things haven't gone right and he feels that they should have gone right. If he ever gets upset it's always when he feels that the team has been ineffi- cient, hasn't done its job properly, hasn't done its recce properly. I don't blame him. If he's left standing in a drizzle because we can't find our way because we haven't been here for months . . .

As you might imagine, the travel programmes take an enormous amount of planning and scheming. That's why they look so relaxed. A team – researchers and usually Mills – goes out to all the places on the itinerary to find out what the story is. They make copious notes and plan it all meticulously. Can you imagine what would hap- pen if they went everywhere 'blind'?

On one famous occasion filming *Full Circle* up in Alaska, we were walking up and down a street, trying to find the right door, and all the doors looked identical. He said, 'This is a fuck-up, this is an absolute fuck-up!' and he got very angry. It was the only time I've ever seen him do this, but about an hour later, when he'd calmed down a bit, he was most apologetic. One other, lesser time was the only other time I've seen Michael snap and it was something so trivial I can hardly remember it. We were off the coast of Chile on a boat and he got caught in the wrong level and ended up with all the lorries . . .

And he never gets angry or frustrated with locals? He never does that 'star' thing – 'I want to be alone'?

I've not seen it. He's always available, always ready to sign autographs, and actually people are very thoughtless, they thrust horrible dirty little scraps of paper at him and expect him to find a pen. He always obliges them and I think, 'My God, that's the price of fame.' It's not something that I'd enjoy very much, but he always says, 'Who shall I say it's to?'

This is beginning to sound too good to be true. 'I feel a bit like Pontius Pilate with Jesus,' said Mills:

I find no fault in this man. I'm quite a critical person. I seek out flaws in my fellow human beings – it's usually reassuring – but I really can't with Michael. I find him good company, humorous, generous, funny, successful . . . All of those things are true, and beyond that, what can I say? I don't know who else you're going to talk to, but they'll all say the same. And he's hard-working. A lot of these presenters are not hard-working. You have to do the work and they take it as theirs.

But not Michael?

No. The only thing I could say is that maybe he can afford to be so nice because, quite shrewdly, he's surrounded himself with good people. He's got a very tough agent, for example. I've never had to negotiate with her, but people who do are terrified of her. The BBC is terrified of her. I'm not sure that Michael could be as totally nice as he is unless there was someone a little bit harder in his camp.

Is there a picture in the attic, that Dorian Gray thing? 'Well, there might be a picture in the attic, I suppose, but I've worked with him a long time and I've never found it.'

Since coming down from Oxford in 1965, everything Michael Palin has touched has turned to gold. From working as a journeyman writer for David Frost to watching the bulls charge around Pamplona, he's been blessed with the gift of success. As a consequence, he's been one of the most successful British entertainers of his age, though Palin clearly has reservations about the 's' word.

I wouldn't know how you would quantify that. How you would use the word 'success'? I mean, I always try to avoid that word like the plague. We met a guy on holiday once called Martyn Lewis who was writing a book about success and he asked if he could talk to me. I said he could talk to me about anything but success, because it's such a dangerous word. So he came and he talked to me and some while later a great big fat book came out called *Success* . . . and I don't think it was one.

I can see what he was trying to do, but it's asking for trouble – you'll never get a satisfactory answer. He was looking for the secret, and the secret that makes me successful is, I think, that I've never ever believed in success, never believed I've made it. I'm always finding out and learning something new and approaching something in a different way. I don't think there's a pinnacle you suddenly find yourself standing on and that's that. Of course, there are certain moments when you suddenly feel, 'My God, that's worked.' But not that many.

But on almost any terms, Palin is successful. He could just turn up and do almost anything on television and ten million people would watch.

Well, that's not true. With *Hemingway's Adventure*, for example, we only had five million, which was quite a drop on the previous programmes. That's what I mean, you have to be terribly careful about assuming these things and I never would assume that. What I think you mean is that people come to me expecting that I'll only do something that has a certain quality to it. And that's great. I'm pleased about that because I've tried to avoid doing 'crap' as much as possible. I think that when I'm approached, the sort of things that I get sent now are of a reasonably high standard. Things that interest me a lot.

When I look back, I consider myself extremely lucky to have worked with Alan Bennett on one of his only screenplays, *A Private Function*, on one of Alan Bleasdale's series and on what was probably John Cleese's most successful film, *A Fish Called Wanda*. All of these are things of such a high standard. I suppose if you can measure success, the fact that I was asked by people I admire to work with them means I must have got somewhere.

On the other hand, I look at people – successful actors, writers – and think those are the sort of people I can never quite be. Any of them. What is true is that I will not identify with any one particular aspect of what I've done, so that feeling of 'Michael Palin – he can talk about anything' has never gone away. Usually that's something you lose as you become more famous, but perhaps it's because I didn't want to lose it that it's still there. I avoid programmes where I have to make judgements, and if a director says, 'Now, in the next three minutes I want you to talk about exactly what you think about the situation in this country', I'll say, 'Well, actually, this is not the way I want to do it.'

When we first started *Around the World in Eighty Days*, we had a lot of set-up interviews. Interviews with the local man, the captain of a ship . . . I wasn't very good at that, it didn't work out terribly well. The people were unrelaxed in an interview situation, I was unrelaxed. So instead of sitting down in a room, I talked to people on the job, as they were doing their job. Which is much, much better.

That's much more interesting, isn't it, because that's how it happens in real life?

It's probably the key to what I do in a way, the way I approach things. As soon as something becomes artificial, I become artificial. Maybe even acting on film. I love watching movies and I'd like to do more, but there is something artificial about them. The large number of people involved. The fact that it's almost more important how you're standing than the line you're saying. So you have to play a role. You're driven up in a long, large car. I like comfort. I just don't like all that clutter.

All that clutter. All the trappings. The 'long large car'. The premières. The red velvet rope. Palin is famously sorted in his attitude to stardom and fame. 'I'm not anti-stardom, I'm just not doing that myself. I can't do it very well, it's not me. A lot of relationships I have are like that too. Everyone I'm close to resists that too. They're very much feet-on-the-ground people.'

Maybe that's one of the reasons why Palin's become such a popular character, such a fixture in our lives. He's seen as someone who's always stayed true to himself. He's tasted the fruits of celebrity – and he's resisted. He lives where he lives, goes where he goes, does what he does. It's all very ordinary. Just like a proper person. For someone who has such a high profile, Michael Palin has maintained an enviably low profile.

We were lucky in that the media is much more greedy now than when we started doing *Python*. If you're good on television, you've got to be good outside. You've got to go on book signings, be out and be visible. We were able, during *Python*, to keep a low profile. People didn't know much about us and really weren't very interested.

The trick that Palin's pulled off is that he's maintained it. The world has changed and the demands on celebrities have changed, but he hasn't – or appears not to have – changed. To stay at the forefront of the entertainment world for thirty years and still remain quite anonymous is a rare achievement. To have done so in the face of such sustained frontline success . . . Maybe this appeals to a very British sense of decency. We could say that it's because he's got the financial freedom to do whatever he wants that he has the freedom to resist celebrity. There's a certain logic to that – people tend to crave fame more on the way up – but it's a rare thing.

I suppose the truth is that I'm just not very interested in all that. I feel personally that all I want to do is my work and for my work to be as good as possible, and to be as popular as possible, so I'm prepared to work as hard as I can at what I do. Not grumble about it. I haven't done any advertising. I don't do anything else. I'm just asking to be judged on the work that I do. Other than that, I just want to be me and to carry on living the way I've always lived. I could do press conferences, go on game shows, be a guest on *Have I Got News For You*, that kind of thing. But I don't want that.

Is it a control deal, is that why he wouldn't do a programme like *Have I Got News for You*?

Yes, it's partly that, but it's more that I just don't want to be everywhere. I actually love *Have I Got News for You*, I really enjoy watching it. The standard of humour is pretty good, really sharp. But I like it as a spectator, it's my time off. I just want to do what I do and do it well. The fame side of it is a bit of a liability, which can twist and distort what you are and what you do. If you're not very careful, you can put yourself into a corner and be trapped. I'm quite aware you can't get away from being a celebrity, but I just try to structure my life the best I can and do varied kinds of work.

Occasionally you'll find Palin going out of character, doing things that would seem to encroach on his personal privacy. Going through the newspaper cuttings as part of the research for this book, I found a few articles on being a father, a few on coping with Helen's illness and one rather sweet article of the 'Me and My Shoes: How We Met' variety. Inevitably headlined 'Have I Got News for You?', it was about Michael and his newsagent in Gospel Oak. There's a picture of Michael behind the counter with Mash Patel: 'People talk about going abroad and finding these lovely little shops where the owner takes you round the back and gives you a cup of coffee as if that sort of thing never happens in England – but it does. I can spend hours chatting away in a place like the delicatessen and I always have a good laugh whenever I pop into the dry-cleaners.'

Being in Control

The word that comes to mind more and more with Michael Palin is 'control'. I don't mean in the 'control freak' sense, which is often just a euphemism for 'unreasonably domineering'. Palin doesn't want to dominate people and situations; he just wants to know that things are secure, that he can trust those he works with not to do anything that might upset the equilibrium. Just as he likes to control his emotional life, so he likes to control the work he does. OK, so in his travel programmes he puts himself in ridiculously dangerous situations, but he's with people he trusts absolutely. He's worked with them for years and knows them as professionals and as people.

> You're right, and that's why I don't do cameos and little bits in films. I don't always feel comfortable just dropping in and doing a little bit here or there. There's always the danger that you'll do your couple of days and they will appear as a sort of fragment of the film.

For the same reasons, Palin doesn't get much involved in adverts. He has done a number of charity one-man shows, but his charity work is carried out without fuss, supporting causes for which he feels something. For example, he does a lot of work for a charity supporting the families of prisoners – 'Why should they suffer?' – and has set up the Michael Palin Centre for children who stammer. 'A lot of things now, you can just put your name to and that's as far as your involvement goes. I know that's true, but I prefer to do these one-night things where I'm in control. I choose the cause. I'd rather do that. That's more in my control, and something I enjoy doing rather than just standing on a platform with thirty other people.'

Adverts are a slightly different kettle of fish. Apart from a few long-lost ads he did back in the sixties when he was skint, he's never done any commercials – and you can imagine how often he's been asked. That nice, smiley Michael Palin? He would shift

Out on the town with Helen, childhood sweetheart and lifelong companion

your products, no question. Partly it's that Palin, for all his current disillusion with the Blair regime, is a lifelong Labour Party man. And it's not as if he's short of cash . . .

I've never been too sure what to do with my money. We've bought little flats for the children, but that's about it really. Once we talked about getting a weekend retreat. I would blather on about it a bit and the children would say, 'Dad's in castle-by-the-stream mode again'. But we're rather happy here.

I've never really been one for grand houses or swimming-pools. Creative success is what matters. Wealth buys the freedom to do what I want. I hate the life of tycoonery. The idea of acquiring lots of material possessions and being forced to have a house bristling with security is a nightmare.

Michael in early 'dad' mode with Will, Rachel and Tom

The Palin Family

Michael Palin met his wife Helen on Southwold Beach in Suffolk during the school holidays when he was sixteen. 'It began as a holiday thing. We didn't see each other for a year after that first holiday, then it was two years before we saw each other again. Then I went to Oxford and during my university years I stayed faithful . . . mentally. We were not betrothed then. We each had free time but the relationship with Helen was the one that stayed.'

In 1966, when he was twenty-two, they got married. They bought their first house in 1968 in a small four-house cul-de-sac in Gospel Oak, near Hampstead Heath, in north London, for £12,000 – and they've lived there ever since. Like most mega-rich celebrities, Palin has used his wealth to buy other houses. However, unlike most mega-rich celebrities, the houses that he's bought have all been in the same road.

There are three Palin children – Tom, thirty-two, who's involved in music, Will, thirty, an architectural historian, and Rachel, twenty-six, who works for the BBC. The Palins made a great effort to raise their children like ordinary children and gave them all a local state education – 'Not through any great ideological stance, but because the schools were good. It just seemed sensible. Why have all those convoluted car runs?' By all accounts, family life is warm, secure and happy. Michael and Helen live their own lives together, and give each other a lot of freedom. 'I have observed it often. The more independence there is in a marriage, the longer it survives.'

The great sadness in his life concerns the suicide of his sister, Angela, in 1987. Although she had tendencies to depression, her death at the age of fifty-two was a great shock. 'On the surface she was very happy – a good marriage, three children, a nice house – sociable, popular, talented. Yet underneath was a terrible feeling of inadequacy. I cannot begin to understand the depths of it.' It was even more perplexing for Michael because they'd been out together the night before she died. 'She had been on great form. Earlier she had said she was unhappy. The next minute she was saying "Let's go out". The inexplicable nature of what happened still preoccupies me.'

He has no reticence talking about it.

I have very fond memories of my sister. Not talking about her somehow makes her a non-person. For me, she is still there. The first thing I did after her death was to read up about suicide. I wanted to try and discover some kind of clue, some chemical reason why someone who had always seemed so happy would want to take their life. She was not miserable, wretched or awkward. I've read a lot now about people who have suffered from depression. People with great skills and talent have taken their own lives. Ernest Hemingway was one. It's ironic that my sister, who killed herself, looked sane and I appeared mad because I was one of the *Python* team.

Chapter Two

Alone Together

Ted and Mary Palin lived in 26 Whitworth Street in Ranmoor, a middle-class area of Sheffield. Mary's father had been the High Sheriff of Oxfordshire for a while, and Ted's father was a doctor. Their wedding was a big society affair, covered in the press. Mary had been presented at court. But that was in the twenties and in the thirties, when the Depression came, they were hit quite badly. They were forced to go north, away from their native Oxfordshire, to find work. They went first to Hull, then Leeds and then Sheffield. It was all somewhat of a strain for Ted. He'd had the proper upbringing – public school, Cambridge – and his expectations were that he would live very comfortably. But he never lived comfortably. Their expectations of a prosperous and upper-middle-class way of life never really materialized.

The Palins already had a daughter, Angela, and by the time she was eight years old they wanted a second child. Ted, a civil engineer, and not a very well-paid civil engineer at that, was worried about the cost. But Mary, who was in her late thirties and didn't care that much about the financial implications, was more single-minded, and on Wednesday 5 May 1943 Michael Edward Palin came into the world. It was wartime and Ted found himself helping the war effort – working for a toilet-paper manufacturer. Not, maybe, what he'd been bred for, and while he soon moved to a steel company called Edgar Allen & Co, life was still something of a disappointment for Ted. If it was a hard time, well, that was just because times were hard. There was still rationing, and the euphoria of winning the war had given way to a gloomy, grey post-war depression, but the most important things in life – security and love and warmth – were there.

Ted had a stammer, quite a serious stammer, and that badly affected his relationships with people. He was a jolly man, but found his stammer frustrating and very irritating, and it made him appear cantankerous. He was, in many ways, a hard man to get on with, but he bonded with Michael in the way that dads and boys do: they went to the cricket together, they watched the trains go by, they walked, and as they shared these experiences, both let their minds wander. As the trains sped by, taking their passengers who knew where, Ted thought what might have been, Michael to what might be. Then they held hands and walked home, alone together.

Mary Palin was, by contrast, light and easy going. The family's fallen circumstances didn't seem to worry her and she encouraged Michael and Angela's flights of fancy and made excuses to Ted if they'd displeased him. Mary and Ted had a marriage that was more a partnership than an emotional cauldron, and were rarely caught in a public embrace. Michael was used to that and found it embarrassing if he saw his friends' parents hugging or kissing.

Life sped by. Each summer they would go on holiday for two weeks, sometimes to Southwold in Suffolk, sometimes to Sheringham in Norfolk. The older he grew, the more Michael viewed his dad with suspicion. He was always grumpy and grouchy, always looking at people as if they had bad intentions. It created a tension. Michael looked at him and thought, 'People don't have to be like that.' Michael adopted the role of facilitator in the family, the one who would calm things down, the one everyone could talk to.

When Michael was four, a new family moved in next door. The Stuart-Harrises were better off and came from the south. They had a little boy the same age as Michael, called Graham, and the two boys quickly became friends. It was a friendship that was to last through adulthood. When the time came, Michael and Graham were sent to Birkdale prep school, where they continued their friendship and behaved like schoolboys the world over: hiding from teachers, trying to skive off games and laughing. They listened to the radio and fell in love with a programme called *The Goon Show*. Sometimes, if Michael missed the school bus home, he would run the whole two miles to make sure he got to hear it. He listened to *The Goon Show* alone at home: Ted didn't understand. 'Is the radio broken?' he teased, but Michael ignored him and practised the voices and dreamed of one day maybe being a Goon himself. And when, once a month, guest speakers – missionaries, usually – would visit the local church, Michael would listen to their stories of foreign travel to places with exotic names and romantic connotations and dream some more. It didn't really matter that he never went anywhere; there were always the trains to watch.

Just as all male Palins had Edward somewhere in their name, so all male Palins were sent to Shrewsbury public school. It was traditional. Ted thought it so important that Michael follow in the family footsteps that he spent a third of his wages sending him there. That caused more tension. Michael got through Shrewsbury. It wasn't that he didn't enjoy himself – he was the sort of boy who'd enjoy himself almost anywhere – it was just that, with its strict rules, it wasn't particularly him. He made friends there and got to know some people who later in life would become quite famous, like a little lad a couple of years older than him called John

Ravenscroft. He later changed his name to Peel and became Britain's greatest disc jockey. Despite having been to prep school, Michael found Shrewsbury much posher and it was here that he became aware of things like class and privilege, money and breeding, and didn't really like them much. 'If I ever have children,' thought Michael, 'I'm going to send them to a proper school.' Despite being a bit on the chubby side, Michael got involved in sports. He rowed, like his dad, and he started to think about girls.

In 1959, on the regular summer holiday to Southwold, Michael saw a young girl called Helen Gibbins playing on the beach. Helen perplexed Michael and he felt a little flushed. 'I've got to say hello,' he thought to himself, and decided to throw his beach ball in her direction. 'Oh, excuse me,' he imagined saying to her, before coming out with something charming and witty. He threw the beach ball, but it got caught on a gust of wind, went harder than he anticipated and . . . knocked Helen's hat off. Helen, who was two years older than Michael, smiled the way that girls smile and Michael found himself inside a balloon floating up into the sky . . .

The holiday ended, as holidays do, and it was time for Helen and her family to go back to their farm in Cambridgeshire. While Michael and Helen resolved to write to each other, as boys and girls do, his parents put their minds to the future. 'He'll go to Clare College, Cambridge,' said Ted Palin. 'That's where I went and that's where he'll go. It's the way us Palins do things.'

But it didn't quite work out like that.

Seedy Entertainers

Michael failed to get in to Clare. He decided that he would read English at Worcester College, Oxford, applied and duly went off to the interview.

'Who is your favourite author?' they asked.

'Graham Greene,' said Michael confidently.

'No, we meant someone who was on the syllabus.'

OK, so he looks a bit studious and those glasses have got to go – but a good chap

'Oh.'

'Who is your favourite poet?' they asked.

'Wordsworth,' said Michael, not quite so confidently.

'Name six of his poems,' they said.

' . . . "Daffodils" . . . Umm . . . ' said Michael, as he reached for his coat.

So then Michael 'went to Brasenose, where they didn't ask such cruel questions'.

Brasenose College, Oxford, was a different cup of cocoa altogether and it was where he met Robert Hewison, a mate (then and now) and more than anyone the person responsible for turning Michael Palin from a slightly chubby northern sports type (ish) to a stage comedian.

'Brasenose had what they called a Good Chap scholarship,' says Hewison, 'which meant if you were a good chap, you got a scholarship.'

Michael (and Robert) got into Brasenose under the Good Chap scholarship. No, no. Stay with this. We haven't jumped the gun and veered off into some *Python* sketch.

'They would invite people who might be good chaps to sit for this scholarship,' says Hewison. 'I'd already failed twice to get into Oxford and was coming to the end of my time as a public schoolboy and my form master at school had been to Brasenose . . . and it was generally assumed that I would be a Good Chap.'

And what is a Good Chap?

'Someone who they knew wasn't necessarily going to get a first, but showed some sign that they might contribute to the general sum of human happiness.'

Michael and Robert both read history and were taught by Eric Collieu, a man who's gone down in Palin legend as having 'the last single-bar fire in Oxford'. What that tells you about Collieu, I'm not sure. But when he met Palin and Hewison for the first time, his parting words were ' . . . and don't work too hard'.

Oxford in October 1962 was 'post-National Service', says Hewison.

> If you'd gone a few years before, you'd have encountered students who were a lot older, more worldly wise. Michael and I were both of the age which just missed having to do National Service. We were coming out of the deferential fifties and Oxford was a very pleasant place. Recruitment was done very much through personal contacts and, unlike Cambridge, you really didn't have to work very hard.

Brasenose was what Hewison describes as 'a hearty northern college', which means that some people were from the north and some did sports. It was different from

Shrewsbury, not so class-conscious, not so hung up on background. 'I don't like the Brideshead image of Oxford. I think it does an immense disservice to the place. Bottles of Merrydown on the lawn at Magdalen was the closest we got to Evelyn Waugh's Oxford,' says Palin. Quite how a Good Chap can say that, I'm not sure. I guess these things are all relative. That both William and Rachel Palin went to Brasenose tells you how he views the place. Curiously, when Rachel, who is Hewison's goddaughter, went up, she was assigned Hewison's old room.

Robert Hewison came from not so much a different background as a different world. He'd lived in Paris and Ceylon (as was) and his father, a civil servant, was a literate man who translated books from the French. 'It was a reasonably interesting upbringing and I had a certain amount of cultural capital. When I was in Paris, aged ten or eleven, my parents took me to see revue – a nude revue. They thought it was so funny that I ought to see it.'

Despite their different backgrounds, Palin and Hewison had more in common than not. Both knew all the words to *The Goon Show* off by heart and could do all the voices. Both used to listen to a radio show called *Monday Night at Home*, which was introduced by Basil Boothroyd – 'It was a series of monologues. Very bourgeois'; and another show called *Take It from Here*. But most of all, they made each other laugh. That unspoken, spontaneous laughter that mates have. They had Spike Milligan's *Milligan Preserved* permanently on the record player.

Hewison was confident, cosmopolitan and sophisticated, and it was he who suggested that they might turn this into something a bit more profitable. 'I always say now that I turned to Michael and said, "You know, we could make money doing this." And he did.'

Palin recalls, 'He said that if we could make people laugh in class, we could earn thirty shillings a night doing it in the Oxford Union Cellars. I found I had a streak of sheer, naked exhibitionism and Robert channelled this very well.'

Billing themselves as Seedy Entertainers, the two began to do cabaret shows. Oxford wasn't organized like Cambridge. There wasn't an equivalent to the Footlights, and everything they did they sorted out for themselves. 'The first time we actually got paid,' says Hewison, 'was at the Psychology Society party. They wanted to have a cabaret – which is what we called stand-up comedy then – twenty minutes to half an hour of sketches and songs. I said, "How much are you going to pay us?" and we got a free ticket to the party, a free drink and five shillings.'

The Seedy Entertainers became stars in their own universe, but it soon became clear that Michael was running faster than his partner: 'We could write together very well, but I was almost incapable of writing on my own. I'd go to bed at around one o'clock, and he'd climb out of college, get some more fags and a hot dog and when I'd come down in the morning to wake him up, he'd written two more sketches.'

*He who laughs last . . . Palin was rewarded
many years later with an honorary degree*

Did Hewison know quite how gifted Palin was?
'No. I had no idea. We didn't think about careers.
At that point, it was partially arrogance and partially insouciance. If you were at Oxford, you were
making all the contacts you needed to survive for
the next twenty years.'

'We didn't do politics and we didn't do satire,' says
Hewison, 'because that was what was going on at the time and we didn't want to do
what was being done. We'd do character and we'd do pathos. We did an awful song
called "I Hope We Never Go Beyond the Fringe". If either of us had been able to play
the piano or sing . . . '

At the end of their first year, Hewison organized a tour under the banner the
Oxford Revue Group. 'We got some bookings and did a week in a nightclub in
Torquay.' The Oxford Revue Group also included an intense, passionate Welsh lad
who was in the year above Hewison and Palin – Terry Jones.

'The first time I saw Mike he was doing cabaret with Robert Hewison in some
undergraduate venue and immediately there was something innately funny about
Mike, something very appealing about his humour. Everything about what it was he
was doing chimed right, it rang true, it was funny,' says Jones. 'The first writing we
did together was something called "Loitering Within Tent". Bernard Braden's son,
Chris, had this idea about doing a lecture about slapstick and he and I worked out a
sequence called the "Slapstick Sequence". As far as I remember, that was the first real
writing collaboration we did, and in fact that sketch was later done in the *Python*
stage show.'

'By the end of second year, we were quite well known within this tiny, tiny world,'
says Hewison. 'Then came the moment when we were going to be asked to go to
Edinburgh with the Oxford Theatre Group. The director – and this was deeply
painful – asked Michael and not me. Looking back, they were absolutely right, but
at the time it was deeply painful.'

Hewison and Palin weren't finished yet. 'Our last professional appearance was at
a holiday camp – a sub-Butlin's – for their summer gala. The MC said to us, "Where's
your mikes? What kind of material do you do?" And we said, "Well, we don't have
any mikes . . ." He was great. He got up and said "Here are these lads and they don't
have microphones, so listen up . . ." And that was a suitable end to our career.'

Palin and Terry Jones reviving their early 'Slapstick Sequence' at the Hollywood Bowl

Chapter Three

The Gathering

'Marty Feldman and I were sitting in an Indian restaurant. He'd been working on *The Frost Report* with John Cleese and Graham Chapman and I'd
been working at Thames with Michael Palin and Terry Jones. I said, "I'll put
my two Oxford chaps against your two Cambridge chaps." It started out as
a joke, but then I got home and thought, that's not such a bad idea.'
BARRY TOOK

Do Not Adjust Your Set

It's easy to sit back and look at how the different *Python* members got together
like some Oxbridge version of The Magnificent Seven – a group of disparate individuals assembled to form an unbeatable team. Life is rarely so neat, so straightforward. However, in the case of the Pythons, if you substitute pens for guns and
smart young men's jackets for cowboy hats it's actually not such a bad analogy. A
bunch of talented individuals, all doing more or less (some more, some less) the
same thing. They were knocking about in the same circles, selling more or less the
same things. Of course they were aware of each other. Of course they were going to
end up together.

Looking back at the histories of the men who would go on to form *Monty
Python*, it's no surprise they ended up as a team. This might have been thirty-five
years ago, but remember, this is England we're talking about and in England it's not
so much what you know as who you know. If that's true now, it was doubly so back
in the mid-sixties. That's not to say they weren't skint and didn't have to work at getting seen and accepted, just that it was probably easier for them than someone who
had been to, say, Hull College of Further Education.

The DNAYS crew: David Jason and Denise Coffey in front, the three Pythons in the back

Left to right: Terry Jones, Denise Coffey, Palin, David Jason and Eric Idle

The ground had been laid by the likes of Peter Cook and the *Beyond the Fringe* crew and any smart young comedy writers coming down from Oxbridge were immediately accepted on to the circuit. Comedy – and in particular, satire – was the New Thing and these bright young men were getting snapped up faster than the train could carry them down from the quads and courts. It's the way it is. Whenever there's a new popular trend, people fight to get on board, to get the new star, the new genius. Around the same time, the record companies were stalking the streets of Liverpool, ambushing young boys, hoping that they might have a guitar back home. In 1965, the chances of a working-class Scouse lad getting a gig on *The Frost Show* were about the same as a nice young boy from Magdalen getting a four-album deal with Decca.

These men – and they nearly always were men; there might have been the odd woman, but on closer examination it usually turned out to be Terry Jones in a dress – were hot and in demand. It also helped that the producers who were acting as talent scouts came from the same place. They knew what they were looking for. It was a world that was familiar. And it was a world that was theirs for the taking.

The sixties were a time of opportunity, a time when all the old certainties were falling away, leaving the ground free for anyone who wanted to exploit it. In February 1962, *Private Eye* published its first issue. But while that was fun, it was essentially a class thing. The privileged classes taking the piss out of the privileged classes. The *Sunday Times* printed the first colour supplement. With features on Pop Art, Mary Quant and her 'absolutely 20th-century clothes', the supplement marked the beginning of the sixties. Newspapers changed too. On 15 September 1964, the grey broadsheet the *Daily Herald* transformed into the grey broadsheet the *Sun*. Then came the fun. One week in October 1968 gave a taste of what was to come. On the 16th, Robert Maxwell bid £26 million for the *News of the World*. Rupert Murdoch's News Ltd joined in the chase on the 23rd. On 1 January 1969, *News of the World* editor Stafford Summerfield wrote an editorial proclaiming that the paper would remain 'as British as roast beef', a thinly veiled attack on Maxwell's Czech origins, and it was announced that Murdoch had won. Summerfield found out about the new world order rather earlier than the rest of us. Just a year later, Murdoch sacked him.

Later in 1969, another institution fell to the voracious Australian and another Summerfield was found in the shape of the print unions. Murdoch had long been angling for the *Sun*. The print unions, possibly on the advice of a soothsayer, put up the barricades and did everything in their not inconsiderable power to stop the takeover. On 15 October, after a lengthy period which was more a courtship than a dispute, Murdoch bought the *Sun* for £250,000, having finally received the unions' permission. Up, up and away soared the super soaraway *Sun*. The fabric had changed again.

Everything became entertainment and entertainment became everything. It was all showbiz. *Time* magazine wrote: 'In this century, every decade has its city and for the sixties that city is London.' In 1967, the advent of colour television on BBC2 put everything on fast-forward. OK, so the first seven hours' coverage was Wimbledon, but it was a start. The independent television network underwent a radical change as the staid Rediffusion was replaced by the hip Thames/LWT duo. Academic notions such as McLuhan's 'global village' became merged with reality as the box gave everyone a front-row seat.

As the sixties turned into the seventies, we were one nation united by a television screen. This was the era of three-channel television. Cables were still attached to wirelesses, satellites existed only in James Bond films. We were on the cusp of what was to come. Television had just moved from being, if not an élitist tool, then not far from it. It was accessible to all, cheap enough for it to be a truly mass medium. Nearly every household had one. The days when people would gaze in wonder to watch the white spot disappear at the end of the day had long gone, yet it wasn't so cheap that families had more than one set, and watching was a communal experience.

After coming down from Brasenose, Michael took a succession of what might be described as 'work experience' jobs. He even did a few adverts – the first and last time he got involved in the world of selling. Still, it was work that was good experience and good money. For the most part, he got involved in things that he would later describe as 'jobs-for-the-boys kind of enterprises'.

There are two jobs that Palin took from this post-Oxford, pre-*Python* era that leap off the page, that sit on his CV like pearls in a sweetshop. In 1965, he got his first break in the wild and wacky world of television, but it wasn't the expected break. He went to the West Country and became the presenter of *Now!*, a pop music show. 'The exclamation mark is what I remember about that show. It was very important – it gave the show a feeling of excitement and immediacy that we were all led to believe was hugely important at the time.' This was 1965. Pop music was exciting and England – well, London anyway – was just starting to swing big-time. Palin was good-looking, young and hot. Bristol might not have been Carnaby Street, but it could have been a pretty good entrée into that world. Clifton today, Rishikesh tomorrow.

But Palin was still a serious young man with serious ambitions and being a regional Jimmy Saville was not what he had in mind when he left Brasenose.

> What I had to do was fairly humiliating, like walking around Bristol dressed in a long Edwardian swimsuit, with huge boots on, miming to Nancy Sinatra's 'These Boot are Made for Walking'. I'd just come out of Oxford with a history degree. I mean, this didn't seem to be the natural logic of things.

Now! paid £35 a week, a fair whack for a twenty-one-year-old, and gave him invaluable front of camera experience. It might have been a strange job, but Palin found a not so strange way of coping. 'I'd go down the local pub and have two pints of Guinness. It was the only way I could get through the show.'

Above and opposite: in Do Not Adjust Your Set

The other odd job that appears on the Palin CV also took him outside the comfy confines of the satire circuit. Ken Russell might be a strange name to throw into the mix, but it was through him that in 1966 Palin and Idle first worked together.

> I had just come down from university and was looking for any work at all that involved getting near a camera. I had heard that Ken Russell was making this film about Isadora Duncan. Tony Palmer, who's a film director now – he does long films about Wagner and opera – was Robert Hewison's lodger and was helping the assistant producer and asked if I would like to come and be in it. I played the part of an undertaker. There were four of us playing musical instruments on top of a hearse as it drove through London. I don't quite know why we were doing it, but with Ken Russell, ours was not to reason why.

Meanwhile, back in the real world, Jones had become a salaried staff writer at the BBC and had got Palin in, writing gags for people like Ken Dodd, Billy Cotton and *The Two Ronnies*. It paid the rent. 'Terry and I worked together after I left Oxford. We saw each other on an almost daily basis, and that was true from those times right up to the *Python* times.'

Much has been made of the two different groups within Python – the organic, fluid Oxford against the logical, structured Cambridge – and that can be seen in the respective *Python* groups. It doesn't take much to work out where Cleese and Chapman came from and where Jones and Palin came from. (Idle was a Cambridge boy and Terry Gilliam came from Occidental College in California. The first syllable of Occidental should tell you where he nailed his colours.) Both Palin and Jones say that if they'd gone to Cambridge, things would have been very different. 'They had the Footlights, which was an institution, and they'd nurture the talent. There was a regime, a routine. At Oxford there was nothing like that, so it was left very much up to the individuals to find their own way,' said Jones.

More important than their educational background were their personalities – their chemistry. Superior, condescending John Cleese. A serious man destined for ever to be asked to do silly

The Pythons – minus Gilliam – during the recording of The Meaning of Life

walks. A man whose natural gift was tempered by his need to put things in a logi-cal framework. Sarcastic Eric Idle. An individual within a group. The only one (Gilliam aside) who wrote on his own, but he didn't mind. 'Why should I mind?' he said. 'I've got the best partner.' Grouchy, clever Terry Jones. Passionate and ener-getic, a man universally described as 'complicated'. Jones cared about everything and hung on to the dream when the others had got bored. Terry Gilliam. What was it he was doing with those cutout animations? And why have all his films been dark and baroque, curiously medieval in feel? Graham Chapman, the handsome one who died. An alcoholic and a homosexual, Chapman was the outsider's outsider, but touched with the hand of genius. A lovely man and Cleese's 'problem'. And then there was Michael Palin.

Palin was the 'lukewarm water' of the gang, and had an ability to knit together this bunch of arrogant egoists and keep these disparate Pythons, especially Jones and Cleese, as a unit. Robert Hewison talks about him being 'the universal joint, the man who can transmit everybody's energies and keep everybody together'. Sometimes he went walkabout when the fighting got going – 'He's not a man who will ever die on the barricades, but he will die with thousands of friends,' said Cleese – but it was invariably Palin who pulled it together. When material ran dry, it was Palin who flowed. When Cleese left to go off on his own, it was Palin who persuaded the rest to carry on. When the others wanted to reform for one last money-spinning farewell tour last year, however, it was Palin who said no. He had an instinctive feel for what's right and what's wrong, for knowing what to do and when to do it. And it was Palin who provided the initial impetus for the Pythons being together, after Cleese decided that they must work together.

It was like the Beatles. No one would have argued that they were the best musicians in town – it was the combination that was the killer. And if Cleese was Lennon, Palin was McCartney. The nice one who was a workaholic. The one who was, underneath it all, more subversive that the rest. Subversive with a smile. Palin was the one you could take home to meet your mother. (Incidentally, McCartney was a huge *Python* fan and if he was ever in the studio when it was on, he'd stop the recording sessions to watch the show.)

The two groups had been working in much the same territory for a couple of years and were aware of each other's work. 'I'd met Eric at Edinburgh in 1965. He'd been doing the Cambridge Revue and I'd been doing the Oxford Revue, so we'd met up,' said Palin. John, Graham and Eric had been together on *I'm Sorry, I'll Read That Again*. All, except perhaps John Cleese, were what Palin has referred to as 'journeyman writers', running around the same dozen programmes, looking for the break.

Jones and Palin were pens for hire. 'We had to make money in those days,' explains Palin.

We'd just got married and were having children and all that sort of thing. I probably had days when I thought, 'Today, I'm going to start The Novel', or whatever. And then we'd be offered, by Marty Feldman, a hundred pounds a minute for this new sketch (that's between the two of us). 'A hundred pounds a minute? I don't believe that, that's fantastic, so we'd better write something for Marty!' So that day would be spent writing something for Marty Feldman. So yeah, we were real, genuine writers during that time, although the mechanics of writing were not necessarily that we would sit in the same room with a giant piece of paper and say, 'All right, now we're going to make a sketch.'

'Mike and I would go and read them through, they'd all laugh, the sketch would get in, and then you would see the sketch on the air and they fucking changed it all!' says Jones.

We'd get furious. There was one sketch Marty did about a gnome going into

a mortgage office to try to raise a mortgage. And he comes in and sits down and talks very sensibly about collateral and everything, and eventually the mortgage guy says, 'Well, what's the property?' And he says, 'Oh, it's the magic oak tree in Dingly Dell.' And the thing went back and forth like that. Everybody laughed when we did it, and when we saw it finally come out on television, Marty comes in, sits cross-legged on the desk, and starts telling a string of one-line gnome jokes. This wasn't what the joke was at all.

Like most comics and writers at this time who got a break, it came in the form of an old Footlights star who knocked on the door and said, 'Hello, good morning and welcome.'

'*The Frost Report* was my first introduction to the real comedy-writing world of television,' said Palin. 'I remember going to a script meeting every week where ideas would come up, and this meeting was held in a church hall. We'd go along, very junior. Very junior indeed. I remember going in one day without Terry and thinking, "Nobody will know who I am now."'

Though Cleese was the only one who regularly performed on the show – that sketch with Ronnie Barker and Ronnie Corbett representing the upper, middle and lower classes remains a classic – it was a fertile time, a place where talents were honed and allegiances formed. 'We weren't being paid very much for the writing; our fee in those days was seven guineas a minute – that's a minute of air time, not how long it takes to write. We were kind of lucky if we got two or three minutes of material on the show, so they let us appear in our little visual films, it meant that they could pay us a bit more,' says Jones. Eric Idle used to write Ronnie Barker's monologues.

The team of writers assembled for *The Frost Report* reads like a roll call of comedy writers and being asked to join them was like getting a call from the Harlem Globetrotters: apart from our Pythons-to-be, there were Keith Waterhouse, Anthony Jay, Frank Muir, Dennis Norden, Barry Took, Barry Cryer, Tim Brooke-Taylor, Bill Oddie . . . However, the closing credits of the show read 'Written by David Frost'.

Earning the grand sum of £14 a week, Palin and Jones found their spot, writing visual fillers and short film inserts. 'The ad libs were written by us and we did actually get to write one or two little sketches, one of which was in the show that won the Montreux Golden Rose award in 1966. So if we weren't writing much and were getting paid absolutely nothing, we were in a show that was very prestigious.'

Marty Feldman

Although *Frost* was where the embryonic Pythons learned their craft and made their important contacts, the two shows that prepared the way for *Python* were *At Last The 1948 Show* and *Do Not Adjust Your Set*.

Starting in 1967, *The 1948 Show* featured Cleese and Chapman with Marty Feldman, Tim Brooke-Taylor and 'the lovely' Aimi MacDonald, a blonde glamour-puss who hung around the set decorating the creative types. Maybe to them that was the joke, but to the watching nation of schoolboys, it was quite straightforward. It's a curious thing how the history of mould-breaking satirical comedy is peppered with variations on 'the lovely' Aimi MacDonald. It just goes to show, I guess. You can break moulds and defy convention but you can't escape your basic genetic instinct.

'We were a little annoyed at how conventional comedy had become and wanted to break free of that. If it worked, fine. If it didn't . . . no matter,' said Chapman later. Looking back at them now (not that you can because, typically, all the tapes have been wiped), *The 1948 Show* is mostly notable for being the first screen appearance of the great Marty Feldman. 'I can still remember David Frost [who produced the show] when we said that we wanted Marty to be one of the performers. Dear David said "But won't the audiences be a little uncomfortable about the way he looks?" And, of course, it's so funny because the way he looked was his fortune,' said Cleese.

'*Do Not Adjust Your Set* was really the first major, indeed most important thing that I was to do,' says Palin of his pre-*Python* work. Developed from a meeting between Idle and producer Humphrey Barclay (who had been in the Cambridge Footlights together and both had worked on *I'm Sorry, I'll Read That Again*), *DNAYS* was a children's show, but a children's show in the *Tiswas* mode. It might have gone out at a children's time, but it soon developed a cult following.

DNAYS was one of those programmes that sneak in under the wire, one of those programmes that you feel only got away with it because no one upstairs was watching. It was a mad mix of characters – Palin, Jones and Idle, together with Denise Coffey, David Jason and the Bonzo Dog Doo Dah Band – and a right eye-opener for any kid who had inadvertently flipped over from *Blue Peter*.

'We'd do sketches, some of them very quick,' said Palin. 'There'd be regular features. I played a chef who cooked silly things. Then there was a character called Captain Fantastic, who was a little man in a shabby mac who went around having slightly magical powers, but not quite enough.' Parts of it were very *Python*.

We'd do a sketch about shop assistants trying to sell a suit which manifestly didn't fit. I'd do all this spiel – 'The jacket is lovely.' 'But the sleeve is missing.' 'Ah, that's how they're wearing them this year.' Things like that. There was the man who is called to rescue someone who has fallen off a cliff and is hanging on by his fingernails, and the man who is sent to rescue him recognizes him from the television, so he has this long talk about what programmes he's been in and all that while the man's life is ebbing away . . .

While they were preparing for the second series of *DNAYS*, Humphrey Barclay approached Palin and Jones about ideas for a new programme. What they came up with was typical of what Palin and Jones would later become known for. A long drama-driven sketch rather than short, sharp one-liners, and pastoral in feel. *A Complete and Utter History of the World* was the last thing they did before *Python* and bears many of its characteristics. 'We used modern television techniques, to look at a historical period, but did it as if those techniques had been invented then,' said Palin. 'How would a television company of the Middle Ages have dealt with the Battle of Hastings or Richard I's arrival from the Crusades?' So you had William the Conqueror being interviewed after the battle, as if it were part of some sports programme. *A Complete and Utter History of the World* was, in its own way, more *Pythonesque* than anything that had gone before. No evidence of any of this exists now. 'All the comedy had been wiped,' says Jones, the eternal archivist. 'But there was one show that had been misfiled in the history section and that was kept.'

The would-be Pythons were getting more respected within the industry and better known outside it, but still Cleese was the only one whose presence was strong enough to hang a show on. Thames wanted the *Do Not Adjust Your Set* team to do an adult version of the show, but Cleese had an offer on the table from the BBC to do his own series and he wanted to work with Palin. 'Graham and I, towards the end of Thursday afternoons, had formed a habit of turning on the television to watch *Do Not Adjust Your Set*, which was much the funniest thing on television,' said Cleese. 'Although it was a kid's show, it was really funny stuff. We knew these guys, although we'd not spent much time with them, and I picked out Palin as a performer and asked him to be in a show called *How to Irritate People* that I was doing with Frost.'

'Mike was the connecting element between our two different groups,' says Terry Gilliam. 'I think that's possibly true,' says Terry Jones now. 'But the first thing I remember is John ringing up and saying, "How about doing something together?" Basically he was asking Mike, and Mike and I went as a package.' Palin remembers it the same way. 'I got a phone call from John one evening, asking what we were all doing. He was kicking his heels and said, "Why don't we all do something together?"'

Barry Took, who had become adviser to the BBC comedy department, had an 'in' with Michael Mills, the head of comedy at the BBC, and provided the door. 'He got us in to talk with Michael Mills and we just had a meeting. The BBC suddenly said, "Well, you can have thirteen shows for the late-night slot," and then left the room.'

And that was that. On 5 October 1969, *Monty Python's Flying Circus* came into the world.

Chapter Four

'It's . . .'

The Pythons – Cleese to a lesser degree, given that he was already a star of sorts – knew that this was their chance. It was their time, the logical conclusion to everything they'd been doing since coming to London. 'There was definitely that feeling,' says Palin. 'It wasn't so much a now or never, but there was that feeling that this is our time.' Even if they'd never done *Python*, or even if it had bombed, you can't help but feel they'd have all been successful anyway, but this was a chance in a lifetime. The amount of freedom they were given by the BBC was unprecedented – even if there was a body of opinion within the Corporation that thought them – it – a waste of time and money. Not that they gave them much money. The original budget was £5,000 a show. And when the suits got wind of Gilliam's involvement . . . 'An animator? Who wants an animator? There are no animators in programmes. What's an animator going to do, for God's sake? Are you going to make a cartoon or a comedy show for adults?'

Whatever their differences in background and approach, the one thing they all agreed on was a collective obsession with Spike Milligan, and, in the spirit of Milligan, they all felt the need to break free of convention. Since the days of *Frost*, Cleese had been frustrated by what he called 'the tyranny of the punchline'. In *The 1948 Show*, sometimes you'd get a sketch that was obviously going nowhere and would end with the lovely Aimi MacDonald walking on and saying something like, 'Well, that was a funny sketch, wasn't it?' It's not even a hop and a skip from that to the Colonel – Graham Chapman in a military uniform – walking on and declaring the sketch to be just too silly.

The initial discussions between the group centred on something much more basic than 'the tyranny of the punchline' or any of that theoretical stuff. What should they call the show? There are sixty-eight documented possible titles for *Python* – *Owl Stretching Time*, *Gwen Dibley's Flying Circus*, *Arthur Megapode's Cheap Show*, *Vaseline Parade*, *The Year of the Stoat*, *The Plastic Mac Show* . . . And though *Monty*

Python's Flying Circus now seems absolutely perfect, there was no good reason why *Monty Python* should have been more perfect than *Gwen Dibley*, which was Michael's favourite.

> There actually was a Gwen Dibley. She seemed the sort of person who would be miles away from anyone who would watch a *Python* show. It was in one of my wife's mother's magazines, one of these Women's Institute monthly gatherings where someone talked about flower displays. At the end it said '. . . and Gwen Dibley accompanied on the piano'. I just thought it was a nice idea to give someone their own show – even though they didn't know it. The satisfaction of someone getting their copy of the *Radio Times* and the children of Gwen Dibley discovering it first – the sheer, stunned surprise that their mother had been given her own show without her knowing it – it appealed to us greatly.

Some names do seem definitely wrong – could you imagine sitting there and reading about Michael Palin and the other Megapodes? – and you can't help but feel that even in 1969 *Vaseline Parade* might have given the wrong impression.

The title apart, the biggest decisions concerned the look of the show. Jones, who'd first been alerted to the possibilities of film and how the look of a show could influence the comedy when he worked with Tony Palmer, was the most concerned about feel and structure, while Cleese and Chapman remained relatively unfussed. Relatively.

> We never really discussed it all that much. John, Eric and Graham weren't particularly interested in the shape of the show, they were much more interested in the material, making sure that the sketches were funny. My big hero is Buster Keaton, because he made comedy look beautiful; he took it seriously. He didn't say, 'Oh, it's comedy, so we don't need to bother about the way it looks.' The way it looks is crucial, particularly because we were doing silly stuff. It had to have an integrity to it.

If there was one situation that illustrated the difference between the two sides, it concerned the choice of director. Essentially, on the one side you had Ian MacNaughton, a maverick Scot who'd been working with Spike Milligan on *Q5*, and on the other there was John Howard Davies, who, as all trivia-heads know, was Oliver Twist in David Lean's classic film and who was seen as more 'proper'. 'We had a few battles over the choice of director, because in those early meetings some of us had found John Howard Davies to be completely wrong for the ethos of *Python*. He

Palin offers to save Cleese the taxi fare

represented the most conventional, conservative side of BBC comedy.' Palin's use of the phrase 'some of us' shows where his heart was. 'I remember a couple of fights over that – well, not fights, but polite disagreements.' Cleese subsequently used Howard Davies to direct *Fawlty Towers*.

'So I was thinking about the shape of the show when I saw Spike Milligan's *Q5* and he'd done it,' relates Jones. 'Sketches would start and drift into other sketches, things would drift into other things. He made it so clear that we'd been writing in clichés all this time and that however much we dressed it up, what we'd been doing was still very much the shape of a traditional English revue.'

What could they do to be different, to escape from the shadow of the man they all felt creatively indebted to? Milligan, who later developed a habit of referring to the Pythons as his 'nephews', had again gone where no one else dared go. Inspiration came from the one member of *Python* who represented something completely different from anything else that had been going on. Possibly coincidentally, it came from the only non-Oxbridge source.

'I think Gilliam was crucially important to *Python*,' says Palin.

His animation provided us with something else, a different dimension. If we had to bridge sketches together, he would come up with what was really funny material, rather than have, like, a music break or something. His stuff was real quality. The rest of BBC Light Entertainment was really tacky, the sets all rattled and it was all done on an absolute shoestring. Gilliam provided us with something really classy, which I think is what gave *Python* its following once people appreciated all that.

British television audiences – or at least those who cared – could watch *Python* and see the lineage. It was funny, of course, and it was groundbreaking and all the rest of it, but it was peculiarly British. Gilliam was something else. He'd been on *DNAYS*, but what he was doing there wasn't anywhere near what he got up to with *Python*. There, it seemed to be genuinely different and really odd.

Terry came out of the American *Mad* magazine. He used to work for them in New York, under Harvey Kurtzman, who was a very influential figure – a sort

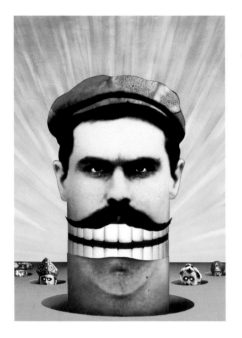

Original artwork from the Monty Python opening titles

of animator with a political edge. Terry learned a lot from Kurtzman. Terry was also into surrealism, furry teacups and Dalí. It wasn't just that it was animation, it was his particular way. You know the foot coming down at the beginning? The great thing was that you could have had something like that happen, but it wouldn't have been *An Allegory With Venus & Cupid* from the National Gallery, which Terry had particularly chosen. I just don't think anyone else would ever have done it that way. And I'm not just talking about one image but all of it, it was so rich. There was always so much going on, and it was always quite savage, heads coming off, legs or bodies, this or that.

'I can remember being in my parents' house,' said Jones,

and suddenly remembering that Terry Gilliam had done an animation for one of the *Do Not Adjust Your Set*s called 'Beware of Elephants'. He'd been a bit diffident about it. He'd say, 'Well, it's a sort of stream of consciousness, one thing leads to another. It's not about anything.' And I thought, that's what we can do. We can do what Milligan's done with breaking up the sketch format and just do a whole thing that's a stream of consciousness and Terry's animations can go in and out and link things and the whole show could flow like that. And I phoned up Mike and Terry and they both went, 'Yeah, yeah, yeah.' And then, as far as I can remember, I put it to the rest of the group and they were grumbling, 'Yeah, all right, well, anyway. Let's get on with the sketches.'

For the writing, they stuck to their traditional camps: Cleese and Chapman, Palin and Jones, with Idle and Gilliam on their own. Again, it's rather a cardboard cut-out of an analysis and while those were essentially the groups, by the time *Python* got off the ground, things had fragmented.

Cleese and Chapman weren't so much a writing partnership as a writer and a sounding board. 'He [Chapman] didn't say very much, but when he did say something, it was often very good,' said Cleese.

But he was never the engine. Someone had to be in the engine room driving it forward and then Graham would sit there and add a new thought or a twist here or there, which is terribly useful. But I remember saying to somebody once that there were two kinds of days with Graham: there were days when I did 80 per cent of the work and there were days when he did 5 per cent of the work. It always slightly annoyed me when people used to come up to me on *Fawlty Towers* and say, 'Well, how much did Connie Booth actually write?' And I wanted to say to them, 'Certainly a lot more than Graham ever wrote.' That used to annoy me, the assumption that because Graham was a man, he was obviously making a bigger contribution than Connie as a woman.

Palin and Jones, though seen as a partnership, weren't actually writing together.

What we used to do when we first started writing, we would sit in the same room and write, but by the time it came to doing *Python* we were writing individually and then we'd read out what we'd got and swap stuff. All the *Python* stuff we wrote like that. Some of the sketches that were 'Jones and Palin' would be entirely Jones or entirely Palin, but the other would add lines here or there.

Written sketches would be read out around the table, and you can look back at it now and, rather in the same way that you might dissect a Beatles album and figure out which song was by Lennon and which by McCartney, you can usually guess who wrote what. The Cambridge set wrote what Palin has described as the 'thesaurus sketches' – pompous studio discussions being a speciality. The Oxford group went for longer sketches that were often historical or pastoral. John Cleese put it this way: 'Most of the sketches with heavy abuse in them were Graham's and mine. Any sketch that started with a slow pan across countryside was Mike and Terry's. Anything that got involved with words and disappeared up any personal orifice was Eric's.' It's fair to say that Cleese and Chapman's sketches were generally more visceral than Palin and Jones's.

Yes, there was a real, terrific amount of anger there. The desire to push boundaries and limits was, I think, probably strongest in John and Graham's writing. They enjoyed being able to shock, whereas Terry and I enjoyed surprise more than shock. I think this came from within, but John never seemed to be totally happy or centred. And that desire to shock came from the way

Graham was. Graham was a genuine outsider, a very strait-laced man who was a homosexual and an alcoholic.

Though Cleese was still the biggest name, all the Pythons were confident in their abilities. But it must have been terrifying to present material in that environment: to sit at a table with some of the funniest writers around and make them laugh.

> Graham and John were writing their best sketches around that time, so to be able to give them something you had to have absolute confidence. Before *Python*, we'd send sketches to Marty Feldman or someone somewhere and they would make a decision and the word would come back to you – 'We love this, we don't like this' – but we wouldn't be part of that process. Here, because we were writing the whole thing and performing it ourselves, the atmosphere was quite competitive. We felt we really had to get our ideas right before they were read. Also, Terry and I wrote more than anybody else but you had to be careful because you got to a certain point where you could see people getting restless.

How on earth did they decide what went in and what didn't? Was there a quota system? Were there differences of opinion?

> With comedy, if something is really funny, it's more like scoring a goal – yeah, that was a great one, you know. There was a very supportive feeling towards anyone who was on form. It was only difficult when there was something less obviously funny, then there was a little competition. Is it funny? Isn't it funny? Can you make it any better? Then perhaps we'd go away with it and make it a little more funny. Then maybe it would come back as something better. But you can't argue in the end, because if it's funny, it stands up on its own.

Eric's perspective is rather less diplomatic.

> Some of us were more manipulative than others, or cleverer at getting their own way. Cleese is the most canny, but everyone had their own ways. Mike would charm his way into things. Terry J would simply not listen to anyone else, and Gilliam stayed home and did his own thing since we soon got tired of him trying to explain in words what he was trying to do.

After a while, things settled down. Their confidence in each other grew, they became

better friends and more comfortable outside their immediate partnerships. The 'who wrote what' lines blurred. Partnerships didn't change, but people felt more confident about picking up other people's work and running with it.

Occasionally, there'd be a bit of in-house joking. Graham and Eric wrote a sketch called 'The Dull Life of a City Stockbroker', where a stockbroker goes about his daily business oblivious of the extraordinary things going on around him. 'That was written as a send-up of a Terry Jones/Michael Palin sketch,' Chapman said.

> They wrote a lot of sketches for Marty Feldman with a Day in the Life of a Golfer-type theme. It was almost a genre with them. So we thought, well, that's pretty easy. Let's write one of those and see if they ever notice. They didn't say anything about it at the time and when we were filming it, Eric and I just kept quiet about it.

Similarly, Terry Jones claims:

> Mike and I wrote a parody of one of John and Graham's sketches. Because of things like the 'Dead Parrot' sketch, which is basically straight out of the thesaurus, we wrote a parody of it, the 'Astrology Sketch' – 'the zodiac signs, the horoscopic fates, the astrological portents, the omens, the genethliac prognostications . . . ' Mike read this out and everybody laughed and it went in. We were amazed because we'd written it as a joke really. We thought they'd go, 'Oh, come on. Making fun of our writing?' But we were quite surprised that it actually got in the show. They all thought it was quite funny, so we didn't say, 'Actually it was a parody of one of yours.' I kept a bit quiet and it went into the 'Yes' pile.

Apart from the daunting idea of reading out sketches in front of your peers, the striking thing is this. The funniest part of making a gag is that initial idea. That's when you get the childish giggle. Executing the gag is almost a technical exercise. Surely they spent most of their time just having a laugh. How did they get any work done?

'Well, we knew what we had to do,' says Palin.

> I suppose it may have to do with our upbringing. Middle-class boys being told what to do. We were taught to be punctual, so actually when we got the *Python* shows, we knew we couldn't waste time, we were aware of that. At the writing sessions we wouldn't waste time. If there was an idea which wasn't working, we wouldn't hammer away at it. Sometimes if everyone was a bit tired or whatever, we'd just say, OK, let's go away and write separately

Cleese and Palin in the now legendary 'Dead Parrot' sketch

for three days, get some more material and then come back together. But on the days when it did come together and there was the basis of some good material being read around the table, it was a really good laugh and some cracking ideas were being made. Well, sometimes it would be near-hysteria and someone had to write all the stuff down. We'd have to go and make coffee . . . On good days, it was really fantastic.

One of the most famous *Python* sketches was written by Cleese and Chapman from an original idea by Palin dating from the 1968 show *How to Irritate People*.

I had told John about my experiences with a local garage guy who had sold me a car. He was one of those people who could never accept that anything had gone wrong. I was telling John that the brakes seemed to be gone, but when I told the mechanic this, he said, 'Oh, it's a new car. Bound to happen.' He had an answer for everything. He would never, ever accept any blame for anything at all. I'd say, 'Well, the door came off while I was doing 50 mph,' and he'd say, 'Well, they do, don't they?' John liked this character and in

How to Irritate People I played a guy selling a car, almost line-for-line verbatim what the garage man said. When John and Graham were looking for stuff to write, they plundered that character. They felt they couldn't do a garage man again, though. I think Graham had the idea for the parrot, which was marvellous. Bringing back a parrot which is dead to complain about it is just a marvellous idea.

Chapman, the most 'out there' of the Pythons, is known for a writing style that often involved lying down on a sofa, sucking on his pipe, watching others – Cleese, usually – graft and throwing out ideas as and when.

You want to know about other sketches? Here's Palin on another famous one.

We'd just had this long day and we were trying to finish off the 'Barber' sketch. We were quite pleased with it, it had a nice manic feel, but we were stuck for an ending. It was such a loony sketch in itself, so surreal and strange, and it's always more difficult to link something like that than something straight. We were just ad-libbing and had the barber say, 'Oh, to hell with it. I didn't want to be a barber anyway. I wanted to be a lumberjack.' And this huge spiel just came out. Terry said, 'Quick, write it down.' And not only did the spiel come, it just seemed natural to go into a silly song because lumberjacks sing songs. The whole thing was done in about half an hour. It was just one of those little flashes of inspiration. We just roared with laughter when we wrote it, so we knew we had something good there. How wrong we were . . .

As for D. P. Gumby:

D. P. Gumby, the man with a knotted handkerchief on his head shrieking insanely, was originally John Cleese's creation and developed for the first series. Terry Jones and I wrote what he said. From then on, he was largely played by me, for some reason. His motto was 'My brain hurts', a line I was always pleased with. We all have times when our brains hurt.

'Sometimes in the morning, when I'm half-awake or just when I'm about to go to sleep, all sorts of strange things will come into my mind,' says Palin, recalling what Paul McCartney said about how he writes songs.

There are moments when the mind drifts and that's what happened with 'The Spanish Inquisition'. There was all this stuff about trouble at t'mill and Carol [Cleveland] saying she doesn't understand. Graham breaks out of his accent and he says, 'All I came in here for was to tell you that there was trouble at t'mill. I didn't expect a kind of Spanish Inquisition.' I wrote that line, just as it was, and I thought, great, what we must do here is bring the Spanish Inquisition into it. So the door opens and in come these people: 'Nobody expects the Spanish Inquisition.' That's really how it was written – it was just a stream of consciousness.

The Cult Grows

No one was really quite sure what to make of *Python* when it first appeared, but that's often the way with something original. Critics sit on the fence, waiting for someone to tell them what stance to take.

I remember there was a review in one of the quality papers, the *Guardian* or something like that, which sounded enthusiastic. A man came over from America, I remember that. A veteran journalist from the *Washington Post* working in London, a man called Fred Friendly, and he was very friendly. He wrote this article about discovering a wonderful show. Then everything just started happening and we just thought, hey, great. Things like that were a little like life rafts being thrown into the water, because the BBC were fairly sort of detached about it all; we didn't hear from the BBC whether they liked it or not. I remember Humphrey Barclay, who produced the first show, with Eric, Terry and myself, poor guy. He came off that night and didn't stop for a drink afterwards. You know, he was clearly embarrassed by the way it had gone. Which was fair enough. So nobody knew.

The whole *Python* thing happened over a long, long period of years and I don't even know really when it happened as such. Obviously, [it helped] that we heard that people like the Beatles liked it and that Paul McCartney used to stop recording sessions if *Python* was on and make all these people watch it. Those were the days before video, you know. And the word came through, especially from the music business, that they really liked it. That was all really encouraging. But it continued to go out late at night and continued to be dropped when something overran. *Python* was the thing they would drop. So there was no feeling at that time that we had changed the face of comedy. It was a successful show for a small number of people. I don't know what the ratings were. Clearly, it never got into the top twenty.

It's probably fair to assume that if the suits at the BBC hadn't liked what they were seeing, then the Pythons – or at least Barclay and John Howard Davies (who directed the first four shows) – would have heard.

> Interestingly enough, we got a copy of the programme review board that sat the day after, which made quite interesting reading, and we found out who stood up for us and who didn't. Desmond Wilcox was one of our staunch supporters, bless him. But Bill Cotton was very unsure about it because he was into northern traditional comedy.

Was there a moment when they became the darlings of the BBC?

> No, to be honest, I don't really remember anything like that. I think the BBC played carrot and stick with us. We always felt we were outsiders. As we walked down the corridors of the BBC, some people would rush into their offices and slam doors. Whereas others would come out and say hello. But I suppose there was a time when there was a certain realization. Huw Weldon, who was head of BBC 1, came to our rehearsal in a working men's club just off the A40 in west London. He came along to pacify us. We'd been grumbling about the time slots that had been given to us and the way that they kept moving us about. I suppose the fact that the head man should come along to meet us all and be terribly charming must have made us realize the BBC did give us some value. David Attenborough, who was head of BBC 2, I can remember him saying how great he thought it was. People like Johnny Speight, John Law, Eric Morecambe, Eric Sykes were fans. It was a definite mix, though. There were plenty of people who didn't know what it was, or where it was going.

You couldn't really blame the BBC for being not so much concerned as unconcerned. *Python* was one of those programmes that the BBC didn't quite know what to do with, and you can't help but feel that that was the point. If the BBC had known, if it had been that straightforward, *Python* wouldn't have been doing its job properly.

> The BBC put us on in what was known as the graveyard comedy slot on BBC 1 late on Saturday night, which had originally been *That Was the Week that Was* and satirical comedy. That gradually became tainted by less successful programmes, but there was still a slot there, where people expected bright young men to do comedy. And we went into that slot.

The other thing the BBC did was bounce *Python* around the schedule. 'The BBC were, I think, constantly uncomfortable with us,' says Gilliam. 'They didn't know what we were and were slightly embarrassed by it, yet it was making all this noise out there.' A possible escape hatch for the BBC came in the unlikely shape of *The Horse of the Year Show*. Back then, *The Horse of the Year Show* was a major sporting event, an integral part of the BBC calendar, and disposable programmes were moved to accommodate it. 'When they took us off for a couple of weeks, I think there was a serious attempt to ditch it at that point,' says Gilliam.

> The wonderful thing was everybody tuning in when *Python* was supposed to run and it was the *The Horse of the Year Show*. In the middle of it, they were doing their routines to music and it was Souza's 'Liberty Bell' – our theme music. It was like *Python* was even there, you couldn't keep it down.

The other problem was that some BBC regions took *Python*, while others didn't. As time went on, they all came into the fold – obviously – but in the beginning it was all a bit haphazard. Cleese tells a story about the confusion caused.

> I had a friend who was trying to watch the series and one week he had to go to Newcastle. He sat down in his hotel room and switched it on and there was this hysterical start to *Monty Python* about this guy wondering around being terribly boring about ancient monuments around Newcastle. And he watched it, falling around, and said it's a real nerve to do this, really terrific, a great way to start the show. After about twenty minutes, he realized that it was a regional opt-out programme.

Maybe because of all these scheduling irregularities, *Python* quickly established itself as a cult. 'Cult' is one of those words that sounds quite romantic but is actually a bit of a double-edged sword. To call something a 'cult' implies élitism and a level of intellectual snobbery. It also suggests that not many people are watching. A small number of relatively influential people maybe, but not great numbers. 'We were put out so late at night that people who had to work the next day couldn't see it. Insomniacs and intellectuals were the only people still up,' says Palin. Insomniacs, intellectuals and students.

There was another group who made up the core audience. I remember how *Python* almost immediately had that school playground status whereby if you hadn't seen it and you couldn't recite the sketches, you were out of the loop. I know I wasn't the only schoolkid to sneak back downstairs to watch it long after being banished to bed.

I wasn't really aware of that kids' rebellion thing at the time. One of my sons was one and the other just born during the *Python* series. Now I realize that for many people *Python* meant discovering your own programme. I can identify with that, as I had the same experience myself with *The Goon Show* and Elvis, for instance. When I first heard *The Goon Show*, I couldn't believe what they were getting away with. The sheer silliness of it, the daft voices, the strange sound effects. I'd never heard anything quite so unstructured. Radio was still the place you listened to the Queen's speech at Christmas, or the PM addressing the nation. Something like that was so subversive. I remember thinking, I really must keep this to myself.

The parallels are uncanny: everything Palin says about listening to the Goons as a kid could so easily be someone talking about *Python*.

Discovering it in the middle of everything else on the radio, that was ever so conventional and respectable, was unbelievable. Kind of dream-like. It was really quite bizarre, you know. You'd listen to this stuff and wonder, how can they keep this up every week? Some weeks were good and some were bad – a bit like *Monty Python* was later. I mean, like, the spirit of it was just something. I couldn't miss a programme. That was something for myself. My parents didn't appreciate it. My father thought the radio had gone wrong.

Did his father really say that?

Yes, yes, especially when Elvis's 'Heartbreak Hotel' was first out and would be requested occasionally on *Family Favourites*. Elvis's delivery really worried my father, he thought there might be something wrong with the old set, that it needed more time to warm up. I remember being embarrassed by it. The radio was something that bound families together when I was young. There wasn't any television till I was about fourteen. The whole family would listen together, so if there was something even slightly embarrassing on the radio, it would run through the whole family. They'd say something about the radio and you'd say, 'No, he's singing. It's just the way he sings!' And you'd get back a comment like, 'Why is he singing like that? Is he ill?'

Did Palin ever watch television at school? 'No. Not really. Never watched television. There wasn't even hot water.'

Chapter Five

Creative Tensions and Marital Fatigue

What happened? In short, it began to feel like work. It's all very well having a strict middle-class work ethic and being very disciplined and all that, as long as it doesn't feel like work. There was never a '*Python* lifestyle', nothing like a wild and crazy version of the Beatles in *A Hard Day's Night* or anything. 'I'm sure people think it was. In fact, *Python* was still quite conventional. I was bringing up a family then, I had two children.' For all the on-screen anarchy, the Pythons were very disciplined. Their working day started at nine and ended at five and included an hour's break for lunch. They stuck with this routine even when they decamped to the West Indies to brainstorm for their films.

> I think people think it was all alcohol-induced, or a drug-induced haze. All doing crazy, wild things. Which is why we could come up with all this stuff. It wasn't like that at all. Crazy, wild things were the world outside: police, politicians, Freemasons, things like that. This is what was mad, the material was all there. It wasn't that difficult to put it all down.

Palin used to dabble with dope but had, by this stage, long given it up. He'd also given up his forty-a-day cigarette habit, abandoned when fatherhood reared its head. 'At eight months, Tom started to climb on my knee for a hug, and it was difficult to keep my fag out of his face and impossible to keep him out of the ashtray.'

There were, in reality, lots of reasons why things began to fall apart. Creative tensions were creeping in. Boredom thresholds were reached. Things simply started to get a little less exciting. John Cleese was the first to feel the pinch.

I loved the first series and thoroughly enjoyed it, and I very much enjoyed the

Relaxing on the set of Monty Python and the Holy Grail

first half of the second series. I was worried by the time we got to the second half of the second series that we were repeating ourselves, though it didn't seem to be a worry that bothered the others at all. In the third series, I'm quite clear that there were only two original bits that Graham and I wrote. One of them was the highwayman Dennis Moore and the other was 'The Cheese Shop'. Almost everything else I could point to and say, 'That derives from that,' and unless you're short of money, I don't see the point of doing that. It isn't interesting. The others simply liked the process, you see. And I didn't.

Cleese had the additional 'problem' of working most closely with Chapman at a time when Chapman was working most closely with the man from the off-licence. It was a problem Palin recognizes.

> John was taking more and more of the brunt of writing with Graham, which probably wasn't much fun. I was writing more with Terry, who was so . . . Terry and I were happy, we just got on with it. Being close friends anyway, for us it was just an extension of being together, mucking around.

No disrespect to Chapman, because the more you read about *Python* and the more you look into it, the more you treasure the idea of Chapman. They were all brilliant, they all had that flash, but Chapman was coming from a different place, lying on the sofa, throwing out odd but perfect ideas, sucking on his pipe. But he can't have been easy to work with.

Aside from the boredom, there was also what you might call marriage fatigue. The six Pythons (well, five, since Gilliam was still very much a law unto himself) were spending an awful lot of time together. Even the most anonymous of offices consumes time and, if you're not careful, you can spend more time with your 'mates' from work than with your spouse. With a group of people who worked as closely as the Pythons, who were so dependent on each other, there were bound to be faultlines. The interesting thing is maybe not so much why they grew apart as how they stayed together so long. Were they all great mates socially?

> Not particularly. There were some people you'd go out for a beer with and some you wouldn't so readily. I suppose we did spend a lot of time together. We'd go out together after doing a show, but we did all have our own friends. But John, he always had another agenda. Yes, with the exception of John, at that time we did socialize together. So fair enough, again it was to do with different characters.

Palin, though he was one of the Pythons who fought hardest to keep it together, now pretty much agrees with Cleese's analysis.

> What happened to *Python* was, we had to keep it all fresh. The first two or three years, from 1969 to 1971, there was a terrific amount of very fresh material. Then it did begin to repeat itself. What happened was that the writing balance went in the third series. John and Graham weren't writing so much and, let's face it, John and Graham's sketches at their best were the best things we ever did on *Python*. I mean, we all wrote good stuff, but they occasionally came up with something that was spot on. Without that, it became a bit weak and then, of course, people start to think, well now's the time to jump ship.

As Cleese lost interest and Chapman lost focus, the onus fell more and more on Jones and Palin. They'd always been prolific. 'I don't know if we took ascendancy,' says Jones, 'but we tended to write more. We were just more prolific, so it always felt as if we'd churn out the stuff and then John and Graham would come in with something brilliant and then Eric would come in with a piece of very witty stuff. It got to the stage where Mike and I felt we were kind of the bread-and-butter writers.'

The most obvious example of the way things were going came towards the end of series three. 'I'm not quite sure how "The Cycling Tour" happened,' says Palin. 'It might have been that Terry and I had had a good writing week that week and John and Graham hadn't got the stuff.'

'The Cycling Tour' was a *Python* one-off. A one-sketch show, it was a conventional beginning and middle and end narrative that was like a proper drama. It didn't even have a *Monty Python* title sequence. It was just 'The Cycling Tour'. 'It was really because we were running short of material and Mike and I had this half-hour thing that we'd written for ourselves,' says Jones. 'We hadn't quite finished it, but we offered it up and . . . It came about through our interest in film-making – again,we thought it would be funny, it would be odd to have a show that wasn't like the other shows.'

Other pressures were beginning to bear. Mary Whitehouse and her moral crusaders were becoming a force in the land and took a very dim view of these young men running around saying things like, 'Your majesty is like a dose of the clap' (the 'Oscar Wilde' sketch). Looking back, it's difficult to understand how the Whitehouse phenomenon happened. There was a short period – though it seemed interminable at the time – when Whitehouse was all-powerful. People who in reality were powerful – politicians, newspaper editors, television controllers – seemed genuinely scared of her, frightened to upset her. It took about three years for people to work out that

Whitehouse had, in fact, no power and no constituency, at which point she simply ceased to matter. Still, the BBC were starting to get distinctly twitchy about some of the Pythons' material. A curious attitude, since it was their job to push the envelope. During series three, they were presented with a list of thirty-two points – things that should be changed – which became known as 'The 32 Points of Worry'.

> One of them was in the 'Summarizing Marcel Proust Competition' sketch and one of the characters [Chapman] had to say his hobbies were strangling animals, golf and masturbation. And we were told to cut masturbation. Very bizarre. I remember going in to see Duncan Wood [then Head of Comedy at BBC] and Terry Jones said to him, 'Duncan, what's wrong with masturbation? I masturbate. You masturbate, don't you?' And Duncan just got flustered.

Being educated and arrogant – a combination that's almost always designed to make you more arrogant – they resisted and got the list reduced by a third. Masturbation, however, didn't survive the cut.

At the end of series three, John Cleese quit. It wasn't really much of a surprise as he'd been looking to do something completely different for quite some time. It must have been a gut-wrenching thing when it fell apart, though?

> Well, you could sort of see the signs well in advance. I sensed John wasn't happy. I think he began to feel restricted by something. At one time he had been so positive, but then it became negative, we could tell. We'd done other things, records, books . . . The books were very popular, and sold really well. But to be honest, putting together the records and the books was not done collectively, the way we'd done the TV shows. It became a bit stretched and certainly people got stuck with the same tasks, and that's when the resentments started.

Inevitably, it was left to Michael and Terry Jones to do the cleaning and tidying, to tie up the loose ends and make sure the book or record made it on time. Did they become like parents?

> No, no, not like parents, more like servants preparing a meal. We'd put all the ingredients together and make sure it was served up on time. Eric did edit the book. Graham and John quite honestly were not interested in it at all; they would just come along to the recordings and be very funny.

Did they just not want to do it? Were they just not that into it?

No, no, not at all. They were never against it, the book and the record. They wanted it done, but they didn't actually want to take any responsibility for getting it done because they wanted time off to do something else. I think the essence of *Python* and what it really was came from the two Terrys. They felt that more strongly even than myself, but for John and Graham, it was just another show.

Does Palin have any idea why that was?

Not really. Character, I suppose. For John, it was part of his life, not the whole of his life. He was starting on *Fawlty Towers* when we were on our last series. That was just John. He had other things he wanted to do, whereas for the Terrys, they wanted to keep pushing *Python* into other areas and exploring.

Palin with Terry Jones, Terry Gilliam and Elton John

For a long time, the rest of us were caught between two stools – whether to just give up or try and do *Python* without John. When John decided to leave, I definitely felt the BBC thought our time was up and it was very difficult to get another series going. Because the whole idea of *Python* was to be a cooperative between the six of us, and within the six we had all the writers, all the performers, the directors, the designers, the animators. So we felt very protective. The BBC could sway this way or that way, but we knew it was our little baby. But it was fragile in the sense that when John left, *Python* could have been left behind.

It must have been similar to a singer leaving a rock band? 'Yes. It was, but it was also rather like John was our passport to respectability.'

It didn't matter that Python was a collective. Nor did it matter that Palin and Jones were by now doing the lion's share of the writing. Cleese was very much the dominant force, not only because he always had been, but simply because of his physicality. His presence was such that when anyone thought about that group of people, he was the first to come to mind. Which meant his absence would be very noticeable.

That's true, and John was. Well, the thing about all the Pythons was that everyone brought something different to the mix. Which is why I would be wary of Python reunions, because I would miss Graham personally, as would the audience. Maybe not obviously, but there would be something indefinable missing. Only Graham could do the military figures the way he did them. Only John could do the authority figures the way he did, absolutely brilliantly. So everyone put something in, and I think if anyone had left, the whole thing would have looked a bit weaker. The fact that we did manage to do six programmes and did do some interesting stuff without John was quite an achievement. But we did miss him.

Is Palin glad to have done those six further shows?

Yes, I think so, because in a sense it showed us what we could still do without John. Everyone else had a strong desire to carry on with *Python* and wanted to work together. Those six shows have some of my absolute favourites things in, like the awful family competition, Gilliam eating beans on the sofa. You know, it still makes me laugh when I think about them. So in a sense the quality wasn't bad, it was just . . . well, it made us realize that we could do it.

That was the key. They had to carry on to prove that they could do it without John. Palin later admitted, 'I did slightly feel that he did over-dominate it.' Gilliam became more of a actor, a reluctant one maybe, but one with some style. Palin and Jones continued to do most of the writing and the shows continued to get more structured, more filmic. The title sequence was changed. The name was shortened to simply *Monty Python*.

> Yes, well, it's funny, because although I said I didn't want to do a reunion show because Graham wasn't in it, I was one of the ones who persuaded Eric that we should do another six shows for the BBC. But you learn from experience. You know, we learned, oddly enough, that people liked *Python* and we thought, well, you can't stop now, it's catching on.

But then, on 5 December 1974, it was gone. And that was the end of *Monty Python's Flying Circus*.

'Moistened Bints Lying About in Lakes'

There was still the little matter of the best work of their careers. Given the talents available and the way things had been going, it was perhaps inevitable that if there was to be a next stage of Pythonhood, it would involve the big screen. Not only did Palin and Jones's tendency to go for longer narratives need a more sympathetic – and bigger – canvas, but Gilliam's mad imagination was beginning to be constrained by the small screen. Their one film to date – *And Now for Something Completely Different* – had not been a particularly successful or happy venture. For a group of individuals like the Pythons, there was only one thing to do. Do it again, but better. Do it properly.

In the spring of 1974, just before what was to be the fourth and final television series, they set about making the feature film *Monty Python and the Holy Grail* – a venture that, for once, really was something completely different. We could argue that *Monty Python* the television series, for all its moments of surreal splendour and anarchic madness, was actually made within the mould. It was, at heart, a wacky sketch show made by a bunch of Oxbridge graduates and, for all its brilliance, was following in the footsteps of the Goons, Peter Cook and Dudley Moore, Spike Milligan's *Q* series and a host of other television and radio shows. *Monty Python and the Holy Grail* took a serious tangent.

It was totally unexpected. Back in the early seventies, the British film industry – if such a thing existed – was very poor. The *Carry On* films and Hammer horrors had finished. The only films being made were dodgy soft-porn like *Confessions of a*

'Suits you, sir.' Michael and Eric in And Now for Something Completely Different

Window Cleaner, and whatever their merits, they couldn't be said to constitute a film industry. If comedians made films, it would be the film of the television series. The Pythons had already done that and it hadn't worked.

Holy Grail was a proper film, a straightforward, single-narrative film with a story, a hero, a beginning, a middle and an end. It looked fantastic. Set in the Middle Ages, it looked dark and dank and muddy. The lighting and the filming techniques meant you could almost smell the sodden moss. As King Arthur, Graham Chapman made for a proper leading man, handsome and sensible – even if his drinking had reached its height during this time and was proving a real problem. So what if the brave knights had no horses and their servants ran around clapping two coconut shells together . . .

Unsurprisingly, the story came out of Palin and Jones's fascination with history. Originally, there was this character called Arthur King and the script went back and forth between the Middle Ages and modern times and ended up with King finding the Holy Grail in Harrods. 'I was very much into the Middle Ages with my Chaucer stuff,' said Terry Jones, who went on to write a serious book about Chaucer in the eighties. 'And I had not been very keen on the twentieth-century stuff. Mike had come up with the horse-and-coconut thing and at one of the group meetings I said, "Why don't we do it all in the Middle Ages?" I thought it would be more interesting and less like the television shows if it was all set in one period.'

'It was a short hiccup from *A Complete and Utter History*,' said Palin. 'I was keen on keeping the narrative in the Arthurian world. I was interested in creating this world and making the convention, the background setting, so convincing that you don't want to leave it.' While the basic concept came from Palin and Jones, it was a proper team effort, a collaboration, and some of the scenes written by Cleese and Chapman are classics – 'Moistened bints lying about in lakes lobbing swords is no basis for a system of government.'

Gags aside, the thing about *Holy Grail* was that it looked beautiful, and it was the juxtaposition of that beauty and the madness of what was going on that made it such a treat.

> I always felt that if you were going to have coconuts instead of horses, what you had to do was keep the conceit going throughout. There was no point giggling about it. You had to be absolutely serious. It's a ridiculous thing to do, but it was beautifully played by John and Graham and you absolutely believed that they were on horses. Again, dress people properly, shoot them against beautiful Scottish backgrounds with smoke drifting and all that, it makes it so much funnier.

Before they got started, there wasn't a great deal of industry optimism. A film made by television comedians that wasn't a big-screen version of its small-screen self? The original budget was only £150,000 and even that they couldn't raise. In the end, they went to the rock world – where they'd always been appreciated. Led Zeppelin, Pink Floyd, Jethro Tull, Island Records, Chrysalis Records and Charisma Records all put in between £20,000 and £30,000. Theatrical impresario Michael White did the rest.

While the film was co-directed by Jones and Gilliam, Palin drove the bus more than anyone. It wasn't just that Cleese, Idle and Chapman were traditionally not that bothered about filming and feel, it was more that they weren't there. 'I used to get very cross privately at home that everyone wasn't pulling their weight,' says Palin. Using the principle 'If you're going to do it, do it properly', Jones and Palin insisted that the *Holy Grail* be shot in Perthshire. And it was. Almost.

> The Department of the Environment in Scotland refused to let us use any of their rotten crumbling old castles. They said *Monty Python* wasn't the kind

of thing that would be in keeping with the dignity of the buildings. So in the end we actually finished the film in our production manager's back garden in Gospel Oak.

Apparently, a lot of the 'castles' in *Holy Grail* are painted cut-outs stuck on hills.

A team photo from the set of Monty Python and the Holy Grail

It wasn't always an easy production. It was their first real experience of working together in film conditions, with all the waiting around, and there were some Pythons who were less keen on that than others. Also, conditions were exacerbated by Palin and Jones's determination that the film should look authentic – muddy and dirty and scabby. 'There were tensions,' said Palin.

> For instance, we were doing a scene when we all had to kneel down, rather uncomfortably, while a rabbit is dropped on us or something like that. So it works, and then Terry Gilliam says he would like another shot, because the sun is now at a lovely angle, just glinting off the top of John's helmet. And I remember John saying, 'Fuck the helmet, you know. Fuck the sun. It's late, it's quarter to seven, it's time to go. I'm extremely uncomfortable, that's it.' The Pythons were not an easy group to deal with.

Things almost came to a head about two and a half weeks into filming. It was cold. It was wet. It was Scotland in the middle of winter. The crew were near mutiny. Ironically, even though for long periods he was barely able to stop his hands shaking, it was Graham Chapman who came through and saved the day. He arranged for the whole crew and the cast to meet in the bar after filming. 'Right, the drinks are on me,' he said and didn't let anyone else buy a drink all night. He instigated a sing-along and got everyone together. By all accounts, it wasn't easy for him, but it worked and he managed to create a proper sense of camaraderie. After that, things were better.

Looking back, Palin says, 'I still think it's one of the best designed and directed films about the medieval period that I've seen. This wonderful idea of the anti-Hollywood medieval film was very important to us, where people didn't have even teeth, blonde hair or horses.' At the end of filming *Holy Grail*, there were two things that everyone agreed on. First, no one could believe how good it looked. The other thing? The next film would be set somewhere hot.

During a promotional tour in America for *Holy Grail*, someone asked what the next film project would be. 'Jesus Christ: Lust for Glory,' said Eric Idle, idly. As the words left his mouth, there was a collective 'Hmm' as various Pythons thought to themselves, 'That's maybe not such a bad idea . . .'

'Always Look on the Bright Side . . .'

It wasn't only the success of *Holy Grail* that rejuvenated the Pythons. In 1976, the BBC sold six *Python* shows to ABC in America without consulting them, an action which resulted in the Pythons slapping a lawsuit on the Beeb. They won the court case, obviously. The BBC up against six Pythons?

> That gave us control of our material and that was the single most important thing to us and to *Python* and its future. It meant that we had control of all the marketing, which made a huge difference. It made us feel as if we owned something.

In 1978, the *Python* crew went off to Barbados to write up the new film ideas. According to executive producer John Goldstone, 'The script they came back with was wonderful. You could just see it was going to work.' There was a bigger budget than last time, $4 million, and one of the key investors was George Harrison, a good friend of Eric Idle's. Harrison and his business manager Denis O'Brien formed Handmade Films and handed over $2 million to the Pythons, simply because Harrison, a fan, wanted to see the film.

One early idea was for 'The Gospel According to St Brian', the story of the least-known disciple, the one who looked after the business side of things while none of the others was making any money. Brian always missed the most significant events, such as arriving late for the Last Supper because his wife had friends over that evening.

After a bit of musing and a few script meetings, the thing was hammered out to be the story of Brian Cohen, a contemporary of Jesus's, a nice young lad with a domineering mother (the Virgin Mandy) who, through a series of misunderstandings, finds himself a worshipped holy figure. Mistaken for the Messiah, Brian becomes a target for all manner of different power groups and eventually is imprisoned and sentenced to death by crucifixion. As he hangs there on the cross, contemplating his fate, the song 'Always Look on the Bright Side of Life' plays.

> We realized that the key thing – the way we'd done *Holy Grail* – was to re-create the biblical period so convincingly that if you put modern characters and modern attitudes in it, it would still convince as being part of that period. Once we'd come up with that, then in our reading up about Jesus's life – which we all did – there were certain things which were so modern that we wanted to talk about them. For instance, the Messiah fever. At that time, there were signs and portents that the Messiah would be coming. Suddenly it seemed a terribly clear idea. Everybody's thinking about the Messiah.

Maybe it's the man next door who's the Messiah. You've also got the Roman occupation, so you've got the whole of British imperialism, which was something we were all brought up on. You can have the modern resistance groups, all with their obscure acronyms which they can never remember and their conflicting agendas. So our target, what made the film valid, was not 'Jesus didn't exist' or 'Jesus was a fraud' or 'Jesus is wrong', but that we rely on interpretation, and interpretation is a political thing and it's been used by people throughout the ages to condone all sorts of excesses.

Made in Monastir in Tunisia, on the old set of Franco Zeffirelli's *Jesus of Nazareth*, *Life of Brian* was in a different league from *Holy Grail*. *Life of Brian* was, in every sense, bigger and better.

Was it the pinnacle? 'I think it was the best thing we did, the most consistent. There were certainly some great things in *The Holy Grail*, but *Life of Brian* is the best,' says Palin.

Looking on the bright side on the set of Life of Brian

It's so tight. It just treads this line between poor taste and satire. We employed really good designers and costumes, which was also the key thing about *Holy Grail*. Some of it was filmed in Scotland and of course there are really wonderful landscapes and it's all free. We couldn't afford anything else, but it was very important to us. Right from the days in 1969, when we first discussed how things were going to take shape, through to 1982, John and Graham weren't really that interested in that side of it. They were more interested in writing good sketches and performing well. Eric too was more on that side. He said it should look good, but that the comedy would speak for itself, however it looked. It was Terry Gilliam's influence: he really was the one who paid attention to detail. He said, 'Let's make it look good. Let's not just go to a park at the back of Shepherd's Bush. It's got to be on a moor.' The three of us really pushed for production value. In the end, after debate, we realized that for *The Holy Grail*, the better it looked, the funnier it would be. Which is exactly what happened. So by the time we did *Brian*, the point had been made and there was no need for discussion. We would get the best costumes, the best designers.

Palin considers Brian *the best thing the Pythons did – and it's hard to disagree*

Cleese had set his heart on playing Brian. 'Yes, it was the one exception to the rule about people not fighting about casting,' said Cleese. 'The others resisted and I have to say they were absolutely right because I was much funnier in the other roles and Graham was very, very good as Brian.' After the way he'd played Arthur, the part could only be Chapman's. Also, by the time of *Brian*, Graham had stopped drinking. According to the doctors, it was either that or a life span of less than a year.

It helped that it was a much nicer working environment – Spike Milligan and George Harrison both stopped by to make cameo appearances and Palin said on the set that, compared to *Grail*, working on *Brian* had almost been a holiday. 'The weather has been beautiful, whereas it was almost constantly raining in Scotland, and everything keeps going as smoothly as can be. If this keeps up, I'll feel almost guilty about taking the money.'

Brian was a much more coherent whole than anything the Pythons had done before. Everything, from the story to the look to the writing, bore the mark of people at their peak. And watching *Brian*, it became apparent what fine actors they were. They always had been, of course, but maybe such a filmic film made it clear. They didn't look like Pythons playing a part, they looked like actors.

Palin especially came into his own as an actor on *Brian*, and switched between characters effortlessly and seamlessly. It helped that he had two of the best characters to play: Ben, the permanently manacled prisoner who really loves the Romans, and the speech-impediment-afflicted Pontius Pilate. It wasn't the first time Palin had played someone with a speech defect and it wasn't to be the last.

It's a bit of a trademark, isn't it?

Yes. Michael Palin, speciality: speech defects. I used to spend so much time at school mercilessly dissecting any verbal anomaly in any of the teachers, because you heard them all the time, talking at you. I remember that patterns of speech became terribly, terribly important. Certainly when I was at school, my first attempts at humour were always being able to mimic how people could speak, because I listened to them, day in, day out.

For Palin, playing Pilate was a bit of an eye-opener. Doing the crowd scene where Pilate is addressing this huge crowd who can't help their laughter,

I suddenly realized that ridicule is a strong weapon in the hands of a determined crowd. Much more so than hatred, which breeds more hatred. Comedy just breeds more comedy. It's about people's fear of comedy. That's why people in positions of power don't like comedy, because it's essentially subversive, and that was a subversive use of laughter in the Pilate scene for all to see.

For me, one of the funniest scenes – not the cleverest, but the funniest scene – concerns Pontius Pilate and Biggus Dickus. It's not necessarily the gag, because there's nothing particularly subtle about the name Biggus Dickus. It's just brilliantly played by Palin and Chapman. The denial of anything funny, the way they both played it absolutely straight, is marvellously done.

Monty Python doing a biblical film. There were bound to be a few people who'd get upset, but such a furore? No one expected that some people would get quite so upset. Not that the Pythons were repentant. Not that they even agreed that it was controversial.

'I always say that the film is heretical, it's not blasphemous,' said Terry Jones.

It's not blasphemous, because it accepts the Christian story, but it's heretical

in terms of being critical of the Church and I think that's what the joke of it is really. Here is Christ saying all these wonderful things about people living together in peace and love and then for the next 2,000 years people are putting each other to death in His name because they can't agree how He said it or in what order He said it.

Cleese didn't even buy that.

I've never understood that, because a heresy is a teaching which is at variance with the Church's teaching, and I don't know in what way we're a heresy. What we are doing is quite clearly making fun of the way people follow religion, but not of religion itself. The whole point of having that lovely scene at the start when the Three Wise Men go into the wrong stable is to say Brian is not Christ, he just gets taken for a Messiah. And that's an important point.

The whole storm reached its height with a televised debate on a late-night BBC 2 programme called *Saturday Night, Sunday Morning*. In the red corner were John Cleese and Michael Palin and in the blue corner were Mervyn Stockwood, the Bishop of Southwark, and Malcolm Muggeridge, a Christian writer. The way the debate was conducted made Palin extremely angry.

I was just totally indignant at the level of the debate. I think I'd expected there to be an argument, I'd expected there to be opposition, but the level of it was so depressing. It was just, 'They're comedy writers, therefore nothing they say is to be taken seriously. They have no serious point to make.' On the television debate, they were just pathetic. They were sort of sneering at us for attempting to deal with this subject. And the rest of it was just laughable because people were saying it was *Python*'s send-up of Jesus. I was saying, 'No, he isn't Jesus. He's a character. We have Jesus in the film and we have Brian in the film. Brian is not Jesus. We make that quite clear,' but they weren't interested in having a proper discussion.

There's nothing like a bit of a controversy to stoke up the fires at the box office, and *Life of Brian* went down well there. The fuss went nationwide and although the censor passed it uncut, this very funny, intelligent film became a *cause célèbre*. What did anyone expect from a film that was criticizing sheep-like attitudes? Apparently, there were two towns in Surrey that didn't have cinemas, but they banned it anyway, which sounds almost as if the town councillors were in on the gag.

Palin's most-cherished memory from this episode is fantastically Palinesque.

My favourite story is that Swansea banned it and this little cinema, a fleapit up the coast in Porthcawl which was going out of business, put it on and busloads of people used to come up from Swansea from the university and places like that to see it. So this cinema suddenly enjoyed a complete new lease of life – rejuvenated by *Life of Brian*.

Opposite: Brian always was a down-to-earth Messiah. Graham and Michael in Life of Brian. *Above: Palin as Pontius Pilate from the same film*

In the end I think we came out of it with something intellectually defensible, so I really quite enjoyed the reaction. Because in many ways it made us exactly what *Python* is about really, the reaction from the sort of people who were the inspiration for *Python*, the little petty local officials who close cinemas not for hygiene but because they don't like a comedy film about the Bible. In a way, comedy doesn't want to change the world, and it never does, but occasionally you need to have your own prejudices reinforced. These people still exist, so there's a reason to be doing *Python*.

Life of Brian would have been a wonderful way to end the *Monty Python* chapter, but reality isn't quite that neat. Like the old bank robber who is persuaded to go back for one last job, the Pythons were persuaded to do another film. After all, *Brian* had been a big success, far bigger than anyone had expected. Shouldn't be so hard to do it again.

But cracks were appearing in the framework and before they could think about doing something as intense as a film, they had to find the thread, the joy of working together. In 1980, they were invited over to the States to do four big shows at the Hollywood Bowl.

Hollywood Calls

In America, they weren't a group of quirky, intelligent people out to make people laugh and think. In America, they were stars.

America is very different. They love celebrities. They don't understand if someone says, 'I don't want to go on any big shows.' Of course you do! There's no question in America, that's what it's all about. Get to the top. The idea of living a quiet, discreet life, what's the point? You go to America and you do all sorts of shows and make appearances like *Saturday Night Live* and the Hollywood Bowl, which is a great chance to really celebrate life in a way you couldn't do when you were doing television or film.

To just go on stage and do all the *Python* hits at the Hollywood Bowl was a great experience. The climate was nice, and the audience enjoyed it. But I'm always a little bit wary about audiences like that. They all whoop and scream and yell in a kind of 'we're the audience and we're having a great time' way. Whatever is going on on stage, it doesn't seem to matter that much. Some stage shows became quite bad because they weren't listening to the way we were doing it. There was a danger that the sketch would become stretched.

But in the Hollywood Bowl, you became aware that you were sort of famous, very famous, and in a land where fame is worshipped, that's quite a hit. There was a special tent backstage at the Hollywood Bowl where only certain people could be admitted after the show – The Rolling Stones and Jack Nicholson would come and say hello. I quite enjoyed that. Just watching. I didn't take it all too seriously. It was just something that was interesting to observe. Also, the people who came to see the shows . . . Jack Lemmon, whom I admire enormously, came along to say how much he'd enjoyed the show. But there were also fashion models and fashionable people who really just wanted to be seen at the latest event. *Python* was for a while the latest event.

It must have been a trip. Getting dragged into that whole star thing, being fêted by Jack and Mick and the rest. To a lot of people, that would be quite a head spin, very seductive, but Palin describes it in a typically sensible way, detached and almost in the third person.

That's rather the way I look at it. There were times, I suppose, when it may have seemed to be getting somewhat out of control, but that was more true when we first went to America. We used to be rather disgraceful travellers. Graham rather liked his booze and the weaker-minded of us would follow him – although not at the same rate. I remember once when somebody got very ill on the plane and the crew actually asked if there was a doctor on board. Graham – who was a doctor – volunteered. This was the person they had just been trying to restrain five minutes before – 'I think you've had quite enough now, sir' – suddenly being shown down the aisle to administer to a sick passenger, which he did very well. He was a very good doctor.

In those days, they might have felt like a particularly civilized rock band on tour.

Then, in 1974, we would do a lot of chat shows and they wanted *Python* to be very *Pythonic* and be really wacky all the time, and I was uncomfortable with that. Yet it became inevitable really that we would lark about. We'd fall off chairs and stuff like that and do very daft things which I was aware were not very funny. They were a bit rude, outrageous possibly, but that was it, it wasn't really comedy. So there was a period when I just didn't feel very comfortable about being that person. I loved doing the shows, I loved putting them together, but when you went around always having to be terribly funny and do things in an alcoholic haze . . . I suppose in a way I slightly lost the plot, but not in a serious way. When I came back, I was fine, but when I was out there, I wasn't very happy doing all those 'crazy things'.

Did that ever cause frictions within the group? Were some of them more happy to embrace that life than others?

Yes, yes. It's all to do with different people's temperaments. That's when we really found out that we were a group and having to be *Pythonic* because that's what people wanted. Now, it's so nice. As I get older, I realize it doesn't matter how you approach it. If you want to stay quiet and only say the odd word every now and again, fine. You should be able to say, 'No, I don't want to do that interview because it's not something I'm happy with.' John was very good because John would just avoid it. John would just say, 'Sorry, I can't make it,' but I couldn't do that then. You were expected to do the lot. And we were interviewed by a lot of fools as well as some good people. But I was only really happy when I felt the mood was right and that it matched my mood. Performing all the time wasn't for me. It was just a brief period where I felt, 'Where is all this going? Is this what you have to do to make it in the States?' Most of the Pythons weren't daft all the time. We were quite cerebral people really, we'd like to think things through. That's what made writing *Python* such a celebration. But you can't be like that all of the time. But when I was there, doing something specific, it was fine. There were certain perks, like I loved being on *Saturday Night Live*, and the first couple of shows. Extraordinary people, and extraordinary parties went on after the shows in some place which was right down in some totally neglected area that just had this little hut with a corner bar which they had bought. That was very exciting, but even then I soon became quite disillusioned with that.

What does he mean by 'disillusioned'?

Because actually what we were doing wasn't really that good. If you're going to work that hard with that many writers, you should really be able to produce something more consistent. It was a bit hit and miss. Occasionally, something really good came out. It was the only live show in America and we had this extraordinary sense of achievement, a terrific high, but the actual work . . . it wasn't very good really.

Michael was dismayed by his costume in The Meaning of Life, *but compared to the others he got off lightly*

The Meaning of Life

The next time the team reconvened, it was in 1983, to make *The Meaning of Life*. Again, they headed off to the Caribbean to write. 'The script had a kind of cyclical thing, it was a bit like Buñuel's *Discreet Charm of the Bourgeoisie*, it kept going into dreams and out again. We all read it on the plane going over and I think we realized it just didn't work at all, so we started off and had about three days of meetings,' said Terry Jones, whose baby *The Meaning of Life* became.

> I remember thinking, this just isn't getting anywhere, and woke up with a tight knot in my stomach like you get at exam time at school. I had a look at what I had and found I'd packed a script which our continuity lady had. I'd hesitated about whether to take that script, but I had and I looked through it and realized we had about seventy minutes of material which we [Jones and Palin] thought was fantastic. When we went down to breakfast, Mike said he had a suggestion and I said I had a suggestion. Mike said we should all go home and turn it into a television series and I said, 'What are we all worrying about? We've got seventy minutes of great material, so we've

More costume changes from The Meaning of Life

only got to write twenty minutes – surely we can do that? All we've got to do is get the structure.' I'd always felt it was somebody's life and for some reason, instead of saying, 'Shut up, Terry', somebody else said, 'Well, it could be anybody's life – the seven ages of man.' Eric, I think, said we could call it *The Meaning of Life*, and suddenly we had it.

Or rather, they didn't. 'Everything that was good about *Life of Brian* was bad about *Meaning of Life*,' said John Cleese, and that was about it. Although it made $80 million at the box office, as happy and successful as *Brian* had been, *Meaning of Life* wasn't. It had its moments – and everyone remembers Mr Creosote – but it wasn't satisfactory. Palin recognizes that it didn't take you into its world like the other two did, and while maybe the structure of the film made that impossible, it was a weakness.

> I think part of the problem was that we'd struggled for so long to get a script together. We were writing for it almost as soon as we'd finished *Brian*. And there were tons of stuff; far more material was thrown away during the writing of *Meaning of Life* than any other thing we'd done. Tons of stuff that didn't quite work out, so in the end there was a feeling that we had to see it through because we'd invested so much time in it.

Why did so much of what they did work, while *Meaning of Life* didn't? Palin puts it down to money.

> I think creative work thrives better on economy. More money doesn't mean better comedy. The best comedy is some sort of complaint, or conflict anyway, so it's better if the comedy writers are up against it than if they're being softened up with large amounts of money. My assessment, looking back on it, was that it was the first couple of series where all of us were really firing on all cylinders. There was a tremendous amount of work put into each show, because we said, 'We've got this freedom, and even though we don't have much money, we're going to fill these shows to the brim, we're going to make them so rich.' And then, as we got into the third series, things got slightly more indulgent and slightly more repetitive. And I think again with the films, probably in its way *Holy Grail* was more inventive than *The Meaning of Life*, which had more money. If we wanted to have a battlefield, we could have one with plenty of soldiers. I think that when *Python* was forced to be inventive for whatever reason – a lack of funds, usually – we were at our best.

Being Iconic

Sitting here and looking back at the time and the ingredients, the success of *Python* looks obvious. Were any of the Pythons aware of it being so iconic?

> No, absolutely not, absolutely not. The word 'iconic' . . . We'd have used that in a sketch. It would have been some sort of art critic talking about icons. Probably we did use it in that sort of context.

But you must have had a sense of what it was you were doing.

> No, we were just hoping that there was someone else out there who had a similar sense of humour to ourselves and would appreciate the way we put the shows together. We were aware that they were different and were quite nervous that those people just might not be there. Maybe it was just one big indulgent in-joke of our own and within a couple of years we'd all go back to writing for Ken Dodd and *The Two Ronnies*. So our expectations were obviously not that high and every time there was a little sign that things had been approved of and gone down well, we were delighted.

You didn't see it even as being revolutionary?

> I don't think you ever do see what you're doing at a certain time as being anything other than 'Does it work this week?' or 'Doesn't it work this week?' We'd agonize over each episode. We always wanted to do something better. I don't think any of us expected that these shows – with what we perceived as their inadequacies – would continue to be shown, that some people would find little bits that they liked and other people would find little bits that they liked. We probably felt, in the sixties and early seventies, that things were just going to improve from there on: techniques would become more sophisticated, writing would improve, performing would become better, whatever. We were just part of a general rising graph.

It was probably impossible to see from the inside, but *Python* was one of those once-in-a-lifetime shows that stands alone, with an influence that only makes its presence felt over a period of time. In 1969, Barry Took said he thought *Python* would be influential but not successful. In reality the opposite was true. When a programme like *Python* comes along the mainstream will either ignore it and carry on making rubbish sitcoms and light entertainment shows, or try to copy its formula. After *Python*, there was no one to take up the baton and, apart from maybe *The Goodies*, no one who really tried to copy their sketch-based anarchic comedy. There were, however, the same rubbish sitcoms and light entertainment shows.

Immediately after *Python*, there was a sort of plateau and nothing really did change that much. And I suppose I look back now and think it was our time. We were very fortunate to come out at a time when television was just breaking loose of its old conventional forms and yet had not been taken over by modern technology. So, Terry Gilliam was not doing what they can do now with computer-generated images. He was having to cut things out of the paper, put them together, move them an inch, shoot them again, move them an inch . . . He had to do it all himself. You know, it's funny that I think that's something that makes *Python* rather special. At the time, we just saw it as making the best of scarce resources.

What about politics? Did they ever see themselves as political in any sense?

Yes, I suppose we were, in a fairly unfocused way. We were just extremely sceptical of political solutions on either side. But, on the other hand, we always pontificated about it. But I guess Terry and myself were sort of left-ish. We'd support various causes, like the aid for Vietnam, which we did a concert for. Then we all did Amnesty International. I think we were all a bit wary about anyone who had the ideal and a solution. It would be more about how politicians behaved and presented themselves than the substance of what they were saying.

Today, the Pythons are as successful as ever. Keying 'Monty Python's Flying Circus' into an web search engine revealed 338,625 sites ('Michael Palin' produced 1,536,295 and 'John Cleese' 3,420,975) and the word 'Python' is synonymous with a particular type of surreal, English humour. They only made forty-five shows and four films and it was all a long time ago. Other programmes have come and gone, but none have had the impact or left such a warm memory. What was the secret?

Well, I think it's something to do with the fact that it's irreverent and subversive and, in a way, it slightly benefits from the fact that it's not mainstream television. It's obviously quirky. No one else had ever done anything quite like *Python*. The combination of the sketches and Terry Gilliam's animation; no one had ever done anything like it before. Children, I think, see it as something joyously anti-authoritarian, a bit subversive and totally unlike the conventional forms of television comedy. I think there are a lot of good characters in *Python*. They may be only there for short sketches – a minute, two minutes – but they're quite endearing. It's not really out to be aggressive particularly, or wholly . . . against the world. It has some odd surreal sides, as well as things that are sort of set out to make a comment. It's a real mixed bag, but I think that's probably why it worked so well.

Palin might say 'Now everything is deconstructed to death, what have you got to fight against?' and that's true, but it's also probably true to say that the main reason *Python* is still so revered is that everything that followed it has been – comparatively – so dull. In the quarter of a century since *Python* finished, there hasn't been one programme that even approaches it for originality. *Not the Nine o'Clock News*? *The Young Ones*? They didn't take convention apart like *Python* did, didn't have a fraction of the wit. Watching *Python* now, it's interesting how much like a sketch show it is. Some of it's funny, some isn't. There are vast blocks where you can sit and watch and not even smile, but even when it's not funny, they're always trying something new.

The Pythons are still close, still great friends. There's a sibling rivalry that exists between them, something which flows between Michael and John more than any of the others. As Roger Mills said, 'Michael has a great feeling of competitiveness with John Cleese and they view what each other does with great interest.'

Without suggesting there's any bad feeling between the two – on the contrary, they're great mates – there was always a little bit of edge, possibly as a result of their differing attitudes to money. Money was the cause of what was maybe the biggest split in the Python camp. At the launch of *Holy Grail*, John Cleese (who'd left the group earlier citing individual needs) suggested to the others that they should get together to tour America. Their third series was just about to be shown there and Cleese felt it might be profitable if they took time to boost their profile. 'Presumably he just wants to do it for the money,' said Palin at the time, 'but we have said "No".' Cleese, for his part, responded by saying, 'It's malicious to suggest that I'm money mad. I have no yearning to own a yacht or a Greek island.' If the spat showed anything, it was probably that they were right to split up when they did. Cleese has always been more money aware than Palin, but he was generous with Palin when they were making *A Fish Called Wanda* and didn't just pay him but gave him a slice of the profits.

Cleese and Palin are also the two Pythons who – in the public eye anyway – are most successful, and are the only two who are still working in British television. The last time Cleese had a TV series, it was a psychological study of the human face. (In the first programme, Cleese talked about crocodiles being lone hunters and therefore having only one facial expression – 'three less than Michael Palin'.) As a film director and an academic respectively, Terry Gilliam and Terry Jones work in very different areas. Eric Idle lives and works in Los Angeles, and Graham Chapman died in 1989.

On 7 March 1998, the Pythons got back together for an informal stage appearance at the US Comedy Arts Festival in Aspen, Colorado. They were all there, including Chapman, whose ashes made an appearance, and there was a terrible accident and he fell down and ended up at the wrong end of a vacuum cleaner . . . They all enjoyed Aspen – probably more than they thought they would – and there was talk, but that's all it ever was. Palin compares the Chapmanless Pythons to the Lennonless Beatles.

> I always feel you should never be led by the fans, much as one is grateful for them. Or television people who say, 'We can make some money out of it.' It's just not organic. We're told, 'There is a market. We all love *Python*. You must get together.' Fine, I accept that and I'm grateful for it, but not at any cost.

Even though the chemistry is still there, the Pythons have moved away at different speeds, felt different levels of nostalgia. Following the successful, one-off thirtieth anniversary get-together in 1999, Palin vetoed the idea of a full-scale reunion.

> That didn't make me very popular. I just wasn't keen on the idea of a multi-city US stadium tour where we'd be doing little more than getting up on stage to mouth the words of a familiar sketch. On a basic level, I was worried about putting together a show that was less good than things we'd done before.

Chapman, Jones, Idle, Palin and Cleese in Monty Python and The Holy Grail

Chapter Six

The Post-*Python* Landscape

Strange as it might seem now, the first star of the post-*Python* landscape was Eric Idle. In a sense, it was Idle who pulled the plug on *Python* – after six shows of the fourth series, he said enough was enough. Not surprising, really, given what he had lurking up his sleeve. *Rutland Weekend Television* kicked off on 12 May 1975 and was a huge success. Two series, records and books, plus guest appearances from George Harrison . . . Shortly after *Rutland*, on 19 September 1975, *Fawlty Towers* started. Perhaps the most successful British sitcom ever, it established John Cleese as a genius. Terry Gilliam was off learning how to make films; Graham Chapman battled with confidence and the bottle; and Terry Jones and Michael Palin?

Following a series of long-forgotten projects – who remembers *Funny Game*, a football comedy album in 1972; *Secrets*, a play by Jones and Palin written in August 1973; or *Bert Fegg's Nasty Book for Boys and Girls*, written in 1974? – Michael spread his acting wings in Stephen Frears' version of Jerome K. Jerome's *Three Men in a Boat*. With a screenplay by Tom Stoppard (who later collaborated with Gilliam on *Brazil*), the show was broadcast on New Year's Eve 1975. 'It was one of those things that come out of the blue. I've always enjoyed the book, so to be able to play one of those characters was lovely,' he remembers.

Shortly after *Three Men*, Palin was asked by the BBC to do a variety show.

I was approached by Terry Hughes (who went on to do *The Golden Girls* and *Monty Python Live at the Hollywood Bowl*), who wanted me to do a sort of Michael Palin Variety Show. I just didn't fancy putting on a suit, coming down the stairs, singing with the Three Degrees and introducing Des O'Connor. That's often been the problem: people wanting me just to be a nice frontman, saying, 'Hello, now we've got so and so.' They wanted me to

Tomkinson, worried that the school bully might be waiting on the next page . . .

do chat shows and things like that, and none of them interested me at all. I've seen people like Peter Cook do a chat show and I've seen what happens – he's not very interested in the people. He's a wonderful guest, but not a host. After *Python*, we lobbed ideas around and I decided with Terry what we should do. I wanted to do something different, I wanted to extend the idea we had on *Python* where we had a long comedy which actually had a drama going through it as well.

Ripping Yarns – subject matter aside for a moment – followed on from things like 'The Cycling Tour'. A long narrative, mixing the pastoral with the surreal. 'There was a book on Terry's shelf called *Ripping Tales* or something like that and Terry's brother said, "Why don't you do something about those sort of stories?" So I sat down and wrote "Tomkinson's Schooldays" in about ten minutes.'

Ripping Yarns was a wonderfully inventive series, genuinely quirky and surreal and very, very funny. It was charming and genteel and like nothing else. It was impossible to put it into a box. It took us back to a world when the atlas was full of pink bits, when Englishmen were Englishmen, puffed on pipes and wore tweed. The sort of world that Palin grew up reading about.

Everywhere has romantic associations. That comes from really early on, I'm not quite sure exactly where from. Maybe it's hereditary, or perhaps it was from the books I read, because most of them involved travel and were all set in this great vast Empire across the globe. Everything I read just seemed and looked to be such an exotic world.

I look back on *Ripping Yarns* very fondly. I'm very proud of some of the stuff from that show. I was pleased because nothing like it had been done before. It was really trying to put a very British literary tradition, the Edwardian era, into the form of a television comedy half-hour. The stories all had to do with the imperial or post-imperial stage of Britain's history – about winning wars and fighting, pluck and courage, going out to the far-flung corners of the world.

For a BBC that had been hoping for a Michael Palin Variety Show, *Ripping Yarns* was unexpected. It was beautifully filmed – very definitely shot on film – and looked lush and expensive. And expensive it was. Halfway through the second series of six, the BBC, in one of their periodical cost-cutting exercises, said enough was enough.

Stephen Moore, Michael Palin and Tim Curry in Three Men in a Boat

It was very difficult to get the BBC to see what *Ripping Yarns* should be and how they should be. They were desperately trying to claw it back into mainstream television – you know, they couldn't really see why we wanted to go after Denholm Elliott. Denholm Elliott's drama, this is light entertainment. And so that was quite a battle. We were pushing the limits, the location, getting good actors in, paying them a decent wage . . .

Ripping Yarns also saw the end of Palin's close working relationship with Terry Jones. It wasn't anything personal – as if it would be – but it was just that Palin had outgrown him. 'It was starting to be recognized that Mike was a great performer, so we did the Tomkinson character,' says Jones now. 'I found it quite difficult. I hadn't quite realized at first that it was definitely Mike's show, but I always tended to get involved in the way that things were shot.' It was Jones's way to interfere. His friends put it down to his passionate Welsh exuberance.

I was always there editing the shows. No, I didn't have any sort of training in it. It was just arrogance and, in the early days anyway, nobody else was really interested. When it came to doing *Ripping Yarns*, I was still there, telling the director what to do and everything, before I realized that my position wasn't very tenable. I could sense there was a feeling of like, 'Who

are you anyway?' I didn't have enough clout, I was just the co-writer. I said to Mike either we do it as a joint show or else I won't be in it, and Mike liked the idea of doing his own show anyway – and after all, that was the offer from the BBC.

It was the last thing that Terry Jones and Michael Palin wrote together, apart from *The Meaning of Life*.

'Yeah, I guess it was. We were going to write a thing called "Stovold the Viking", but it just didn't seem to be working very well. I can't say why exactly, it's almost as if Mike lost his interest in writing somehow. He got much more interested in performing at that stage.' Has Jones ever tried to pick up the partnership again? 'No, no. The last time we tried writing, it was as if the spirit had gone in the writing partnership.'

All creative partnerships come and go – two inquisitive minds can't expect to stay together on the same path for too long and inevitably some sort of separation is usually the answer. Whether they can split as professionals and stay together as humans is a tougher question. When Palin and Jones reached the end of their road, it bore an uncanny resemblance to when Palin left Robert Hewison. Both parties knew it was time to move on. More to the point, both parties knew it was time for Palin to move on and that if he didn't, he'd be held back. Just as Palin and Hewison are still very close mates, so too are Palin and Jones. It's typical that Palin should have remained on such close terms with both of them, though it's as much a credit to them as it is to him. Sometimes you've just got to accept that your friend can run faster than you can. Or fly higher.

There's a sketch from *Ripping Yarns* which Palin considers to be one of the three best he's been involved in. It's from the 'Roger of the Raj' episode and involves Lord Bartlesham, a terribly decent chap stuck in a terrible reactionary world, and his wife.

LORD BARTLESHAM: Just suppose for a minute that when Wallenstein reached the gates of Magdeburg in 1631, instead of razing the city to the ground and putting its inhabitants to the sword, he'd said, 'What a lovely place! How lucky you are to live here. I live in Sweden. You must come and see me some time.' Just think what a difference it would have made. He'd have gone down in history as a nice chap, instead of the Butcher of Magdeburg.

LADY BARTLESHAM: Eat up, dear, and stop talking piffle.

Which are his other two favourites?

There's a scene in *Life of Brian* where the Centurion sends people off to be crucified – 'Crucifixion? Good, out of the door, line on the left, one cross each. Next?' I love that character – all these people are surrounding this centurion, Nisus Wettus, who's trying to do his best, decent chap, out of a good school, been posted to Judea, and he's surrounded by these complete lunatics.

And number one?

I'm a great fan of the 'Fish Slapping Dance'. In fact, if all the work I'd ever done was going to be destroyed and I could save one minute of it, that's what I'd save. There's just something so elementally silly about 'The Fish Slapping Dance', it works so satisfactorily, that I would put it on that list.

Making Movies

If we were to say that for Palin the seventies was the decade of *Python* and the nineties was the decade of the travelogue, then the eighties was the decade of drama. Again, Palin was fantastically prolific and produced a body of work that impresses in its scope and range. On the big screen, he starred in and co-wrote *Time Bandits* (1981); conceived, wrote, co-produced and starred in *The Missionary* (1982); wrote and starred in *The Meaning of Life* (1983); and starred in *A Private Function* (1985), *The Dress* (1985), *Brazil* (1985) and *A Fish Called Wanda* (1988). On television, he wrote *East of Ipswich* (1987) and *Number 27* (1988). Then there was Alan Bleasdale's *GBH* (1991), in which he starred. He worked with Sean Connery, Shelley Duvall, Denholm Elliott, Trevor Howard, Maggie Smith, Michael Hordern, Robert De Niro . . . And that's without even mentioning his children's books:

Two scenes from Los Heroes del Tiempo – *a.k.a.* Time Bandits

Small Harry and the Toothache Pills (1982), *The Limerick Book* (1985), *The Mirrorstone* (1986), *Cyril and the Dinner Party* (1986) and *Cyril and the House of Commons* (1986).

Michael had starred in Terry Gilliam's first solo, post-*Python* film, *Jabberwocky*, in 1977, and so when Gilliam was ready to chance his arm again, it made sense that Palin would be the first person he'd call. He'd written a draft for something called 'The Ministry' (which would later become *Brazil*) and another script based on the story of the Minotaur, 'but that didn't get any interest either, so I thought "Let's go commercial. Let's write a film for kids."' That is, a film for kids put through the Gilliam filter. Gilliam outlined the script, Palin came in to flesh out the dialogue and George Harrison wrote the cheque. 'George has a marvellous attitude to filming,' said Palin. 'As soon as he gives his approval, it's just a case of steaming ahead and doing it. You don't get the feeling he's constantly looking at script changes or the balance sheet.'

George Harrison came to the rescue once again the following year, when Palin decided it was his turn to chance his arm. Harrison was one of the first people on the *Python* bandwagon (he wrote them a telegram after the first show was broadcast in

Above and opposite: Palin in 1977's Jabberwocky *with (above) Gilliam, Jones and Idle*

1969) and had followed their careers ever since. A big fan of *Ripping Yarns* (and, apart from the good folk in the BBC accounts department, who wasn't?), 'He said to me, "If you can come up with a screenplay, we'll finance it." Well, you can't ignore an offer like that.' Like all the Pythons, Palin had been working on *Meaning of Life* and it wasn't really getting anywhere. It was hard work, and here was an offer from the gods.

> I made a deliberate decision to take some time off and think about some of my own ideas. There are certain things I would write only in the Python group and there are certain things that Terry and I can do together really well. But what I wanted to find out was what I could do on my own, whether I could write more than just a five-minute sketch and could sustain a story and characters.

Once more, Palin looked backwards for inspiration.

> We had many missionaries who used to come to the school, or certainly they

used to come to the church that I used to attend every Sunday with my parents, and I can remember a particular spectacularly physical missionary, all bronzed and scarred from his encounters in Africa. It was not really the message, but the messenger being a rather wonderful figure and well travelled. I seem to remember he had one arm missing, which fascinated us completely. He'd been through it all. Talking about the dangers out there and the diseases and stuff. I remember that. And I remember a man who taught me maths at school who had worked in Madagascar. That was interesting, someone who had actually been there.

It was 'the first time I was given carte blanche to make a film of my own'. *The Missionary* was the story of a man who comes back from Africa and finds himself the object of people's affections and the subject of their hypocrisies. The Reverend Charles Fortescue (Palin) returns to London and is assigned the task of setting up a mission for fallen women by the Bishop of London. Much of the story concerns

In The Missionary *with (above) Maggie Smith and (opposite) Denholm Elliott*

Fortescue's method for consoling fallen women. He has a 'talent' for helping them, but when his benefactor, Lady Ames (Maggie Smith), finds him helping three fallen women in his bed, she threatens to withdraw her support . . . Palin saw it as an elegant look at Edwardian morals and manners; the marketing department saw it as a sex comedy, and loathe as he was to give in to that label, he saw their point. 'I could just see this couple in the Midwest: "Gee, honey. What are we going to do

tonight? We can either go to the rodeo or see an elegant look at Edwardian morals and manners."'

Starring a host of proper actors like Maggie Smith, Denholm Elliott and Trevor Howard, *The Missionary* was warm, luscious and tactile. Is it frightening, acting with people like that, such great actors?

Yeah, you approach them deferentially, but then you're thrown in and you've just got to play the scene. The really good actors never make you feel that they're great actors. They just play the line really well and then suddenly you play your line. It's just like a game of ping-pong. But also, a lot of these straight actors are bored stiff doing straight roles all the time, playing Shakespeare and classical Greek tragedy, and they really want to play a bit of comedy. I wanted them to play themselves straight and the comedy would come out of that. I was pleased that it was a departure from *Python*. It was more conventional, while a lot of the humour worked very well, I don't think the drama worked quite as well as it should have done. Still, it's a nice film, a beauty to watch.

A Private Function

Palin crossed swords again with Smith and Elliott in *A Private Function*. Directed by Malcolm Mowbray, from one of Alan Bennett's few screenplays, it was, again, a quality piece of work. Typically for Palin, it was very English, historical and structured around attention to fine detail. Gilbert Chilvers the chiropodist was a perfect part. Quintessentially English, with manners and mores from a bygone age, a little man with a good heart, someone for whom the phrase 'mustn't grumble' might have been invented. 'I find that I'm drawn to characters who are failures or losers,' Palin said. 'I find people like that more interesting than heroes, or the accepted archetype of what a successful person is supposed to be. I mistrust all that. I think it's far more important to know and understand people.' It's a familiar Palin trait, and many times in the past he's said that he's not so much interested in heroes as in the people who get in the way of the heroes.

A Private Function was set during in 1947, during the preparations for the 1947 royal wedding. Rationing was still in operation, but a feast was being planned to celebrate. Enter Betty.

> Alan Bennett said, 'I want you to play the part of a chiropodist. The job might possibly entail some unpleasant work with a pig . . . ' The pig was very nervous, especially at the beginning. She'd come on the set and have a crap straight away. Everyone would laugh and that would make her do another one. It was regular as clockwork, a bit like a train. Every twenty minutes it would happen again, but it didn't put me off because I think Alan Bennett is one of the funniest writers of English comedy around. To be asked by him is

Michael Palin with co-stars Betty the infamous pig and Maggie Smith during filming of A Private Function

something you just accept. And to work opposite Maggie Smith . . . it's not the sort of thing you turn down.

Michael felt immediately in tune with Bennett's writing. 'When I read the script, it had a lot of the qualities that I like to put in my own scripts.' It's not entirely surprising – while they're not exactly contemporaries, Palin and Bennett go back a long way and have much in common in terms of background and experience.

For Bennett and the producers of the film, there was another reason to ask Michael. Where Michael went, George Harrison and Denis O'Brien – Handmade Films – followed. 'I remember going to the first meeting with Alan and the producers and I thought they were going to tell me when they were doing it, where the locations were and all that stuff, when in fact they were asking me where they might get the money.' Again, Michael came good. 'Denis and George have been wonderful supporters. I don't think Denis understood it at all, really. I don't think he quite knew why he was doing it, he just felt that if I wanted to do it, it was good enough for him.'

Brazil

While *A Private Function* was, in many ways, a perfect Palin film, part of the appeal was that it was a straight role. The film was a gentle comedy, but Palin wasn't gagging. There wasn't room for any of that twinkly-eyed stuff. Gilbert was a straight man. A dull man. The next step for him was to play someone who wasn't a Palin figure in something that wasn't a Palin film.

Terry Gilliam's *Brazil* was an extraordinary film, from its look to its feel to its subject. Described by Gilliam as 'Walter Mitty meets Franz Kafka', it was dark, thoughtful and subversive, with the inevitable fantasy interludes. It was the third film Palin had done with Gilliam and while Palin puts this down to friendship and 'a moral obligation' after being in Gilliam's first two films, Gilliam is more straightforward. 'Mike's ambitious. He's the image of success and does everything right.'

For the first time, Palin played if not exactly a baddy, then someone with a dubious moral viewpoint. His role was an interrogator and a torturer, and a dubious moral viewpoint was the very minimum requirement. That he came complete with his Mr Affability image added a nice twist.

We talked about the nature of evil and the way it manifests itself. Terry and I both felt that it's a cliché and absurd generalization to think that all evil people look evil, have scars on their faces and go 'Heh, heh, heh'. Often the most dangerous people are those who appear most plausible and most charming.

Michael looking like he's wandered off the set of The Third Man *in Gilliam's* Brazil

One curious side story is that the producer, Arnon Milchan, showed the script to a number of stars, including Robert De Niro, who said that he liked it, he wanted to be in it and the part he wanted to play was Jack Lint. 'I'm sorry,' said Terry Gilliam. 'My friend Mike is going to do that. You'll have to choose something else.' You can talk about friendship and loyalty and being 'morally obliged' all you like, but turning down Robert De Niro . . . that falls into a different category entirely. As it turned out, De Niro was so keen on *Brazil* that he chose another part, Harry Tuttle.

Nostalgialand

If *Brazil* was a typical Gilliam project, so Palin's next project reverted to typical Palin. *East of Ipswich* took him back into Nostalgialand, that familiar place where everything smells of tweed and morality is a relatively straightforward matter. This was about as far as you could get from Gilliam's dark, labyrinthine, gothic horrors. Seen in retrospect, *East of Ipswich* laid the ground for *American Friends*, and was a 'sort of family biography or family memoir', as he put it. Loosely based on the story of how he met Helen, *East of Ipswich* is set in Southwold in 1957 and tells of a family who go there on holiday, where the seventeen-year-old son falls in love . . . 'I've got David Puttnam to thank for that. He was putting together a series of plays under the banner "First Love" with different writers and different casts, shot on film, and he asked me if I had an idea.' Though Palin doesn't appear in it, you can feel him in every scene – from the young lad looking for adventure to the grouchy dad dragging him round churches, it was like flicking through the pages of a family photo album.

Almost as if in reaction, his next television play was contemporary and about as political as Palin's ever been: a story about 'bulldozers – mechanical and human – greed, incompetence, and car telephones', *Number 27* hit out at the Thatcher era and the whole Yuppie phenomenon, both of which greatly offended both his liberal sensitivities and his sense of justice, history and fair play. 'I was reading the newspaper and there was a story about some property owned by Eton College, the country's premier public school, which was being left to wrack and ruin quite near where I used to live. Terrible pressure was being put on tenants to get them out . . . ' The eighties story. 'I was very happy to do it and it was a happy filming experience, but, looking back, the thing that I can really [see] were the mobile phones that they were using.'

Now what's Dad looking at? East of Ipswich, *a reminder of summer holidays gone by*

Palin's feelings towards the politics of the eighties also came out in 1991, when he took the lead role in Alan Bleasdale's series *GBH*. An examination of what happened in political life in Liverpool as the Thatcher administration ripped the heart out of the city, it was what Palin describes as 'a meaty acting role, and it was a chance to see if I could do something like that'. Projects like *East of Ipswich* and *Number 27* were perfect for Michael Palin. They allowed him the freedom to do what he wanted, they were small enough to control, and they let him be as creative as he wanted. But while working on *Number 27*, he got a call from John Cleese. 'And now for something completely different,' said his old friend.

Wanda

Every so often, John Cleese makes something that touches the pulse, that is, for whatever reason, just right for when it was made. It happened in 1975 with *Fawlty Towers* and it happened again in 1988 when he made *A Fish Called Wanda* – according to the poster, 'A tale of murder, greed, lust, revenge and seafood'. Directed by the Ealing Comedy veteran Charles Crichton, *Wanda* became a smash, one of those films that takes on a life of its own, and it was the third most successful British film after *Four Weddings and a Funeral* and *The Full Monty*. Starring Cleese, Kevin Kline, Jamie Lee Curtis and Michael Palin, it was a crossbreed between a proper, glossy Hollywood movie and a nice, eccentric British film.

Wanda made John Cleese an international film star, and it didn't hurt Palin's reputation in that area either. Was it one of those experiences where you could see it coming?

It was extremely successful, in box-office terms, but initially no one was quite sure how this mixture of English and American actors would work. Jamie and Kevin were from completely different backgrounds. Kevin was an East Coast theatre actor. Jamie was a celebrity, showbiz all the way. John and I had obviously worked together. I quite enjoyed working out the character of Ken, but we didn't really know how all the flavours would mix and what the flavour would be till the end of the first week. I think we suddenly realized we were producing some good stuff and that we were making each other laugh. So from then on we thought this could be OK. But big success isn't something you ever expect. And I don't think it did really change people in the end.

Michael with John Cleese, Kevin Kline and Jamie Lee Curtis in A Fish Called Wanda

The other thing that happened was that the success of *Wanda* opened a lot of doors. You star in a big, profit-making film, and suddenly you're A-list.

> That's not particularly true, because the character I was playing was so specific and so particular. People weren't saying, 'Oh, yes, we must do a movie all about the stammerer.' But certainly Hollywood does look at the balance sheet and the balance sheet was good. And yes, realistically, anyone associated with *Wanda* could possibly be brought into any film.
>
> Because the character I played wasn't a central romantic hero or a sort of Hugh Grant type, it couldn't be moved or shifted around at all. It's not really so specific that the role I played would have to be another stammerer, but on the other hand I think there are certain British characteristics which are acceptable, things like butlers. Nice ineffectual men. Occasionally a baddie. So, my cap didn't fit very easily into that. I suppose I got offered films after *Wanda*. But I got offered films after *Life of Brian*. Probably just as many.

Did he just not fancy it?

'No, they just weren't any good. Some were terrible. One or two were made.'

The controversy – and even in a nice film directed by Charles Crichton there had to be a bit of controversy – came in the form of Michael Palin's character, Ken. Ken was a chronic stammerer and some folk – probably the same people who'd been waving banners when *Life of Brian* was released – got all upset about it. Made a bit of a fuss. Palin was annoyed by this more than he normally might have been because, of course, stammering was a subject close to his heart. It was what he'd grown up with.

'I wouldn't have dreamed of doing it while my father was alive,' Palin said later. 'The image of the stammerer is as a solemn, taciturn and humourless figure. This is bull. My father had a lot of words to say but cruelly life frustrated him. We would pray that something would change so that the words I know he wanted to say would flow without hindrance.' Cleese, too, was aware of Palin's background and consulted closely with him when writing the part. Palin answered the critics in the best way possible. In 1993, he opened the Michael Palin Centre, Britain's first specialist unit for stammering children.

Fierce Creatures

Ignoring that age-old piece of advice 'Never go back', Cleese got the team together again in 1995 to make *Fierce Creatures*, a film about a zoo which kept only dangerous animals. It wasn't *Wanda*. (Curiously, *Fierce Creatures* was based on a 1967 Palin and Jones play for the BBC strand Comedy Playhouse which was turned down.)

Getting to know the creatures . . .

Not wanting to sound so wise after the event, I could see something wasn't right long before we actually made the film. It's hard. I felt John – rightly – wanted to avoid doing another *Wanda*. He could easily have done that, and I think a lot people would have been happy with that. Certainly a lot of people in Hollywood. More adventures of the same crowd. That's why you see Kevin at the end, squashed on the roller. John didn't want to write another story with the same characters which wouldn't be as good. So what happens is, you end up with another story with the same actors which isn't as good.

If there hadn't been a *Wanda* and those expectations, could it have worked?

If there hadn't been *Wanda*, it would probably have played very respectably and people would have said, 'Hey, this is funny. Nice zoo movie, John Cleese very funny, and animals and stuff.' I just don't think it was deserving of its fate. But I think if you try to develop from what you've done before, and you hit a success, there are always going to be comparisons. *Wanda* had created its own legend very quickly, and I think the problem was probably that we waited so long to make a sequel, and should have done it perhaps earlier. I don't know, you can say anything with hindsight.

Fierce Creatures was touched by the kiss of death. The production had to break for a year because Palin was off doing *Full Circle* and by then they had a new director. Cleese decided that a bit of tweaking and re-editing could help, but it became a lot more than a bit of tweaking and in the end they put on a new forty-minute ending. 'It was clear that there was something wrong. For me, to be honest, it wasn't a very happy experience.'

Hooray for Hollywood

Wanda took Palin on to a new level. It was a different kind of stardom that he had now. Whether he chose to embrace it or not, he was an international film star, rubbing shoulders with the likes of Kevin Kline and Jamie Lee Curtis. He could have joined the world of the celebrity, going to launches and premières. He could have done what so many people want to do: be on the other side of the red velvet rope. And it would have been honourable. It wouldn't have been at the expense of his integrity or his grandmother's freedom. He could have got on a plane and headed off down Sunset Boulevard. But he didn't. He chose to stay at home and become a cover star for the *Radio Times* instead.

That he took this path might have seemed strange from a career point of view – why wasn't he in Hollywood becoming a star? or at least writing screenplays for big productions? – but it's another example of Palin following his nose. In retrospect, that he went into the travel business should have surprised no one.

Palin has always been a man who has followed his nose, preferring to work on projects that are close his heart or that appeal to his notion of art rather than on things that might line his wallet. OK, so from very early in his career money wasn't a life-and-death issue, but how many rich people aren't spurred on by money?

> People say to me, you seem to really enjoy what you're doing and I think that is true. If I don't think I'll enjoy it, I won't do it. Even if it's hard work, if I'm happy doing it, I'm just happy. It was hard doing *GBH*, very tough going. But I believed in it. Whether these things are brave or foolhardy I don't know. Whatever it is, it just feels right to me to do that and I think that's something that's come from *Python*. It gave me a confidence that if you really believe in something completely and in the way it should be done, and you stick with those beliefs, then you're going to produce something better than if you wait for someone to tell you what you should be doing.

There's another thing. Michael Palin's choices are made under the umbrella of freedom, financial and creative. He can resist temptation. He won't do work he doesn't need to do and he doesn't need to do any work that he doesn't want to do.

> I do feel happier now. In a way, I've done so many things that I have worked hard on and that are of good quality that if I had to stop, it wouldn't worry me. I mean, I won't, because I want to keep doing things. But I've done enough that I'm proud of, and probably more things than most people have done in their lives. That takes away the pressure and the fear and the tension, which makes me less vulnerable to people who say, 'You've got to do this, you've got to do that.' I know it's come from within me and I feel a little more settled now because of what I've done over the years, but it doesn't mean I want to stop.

Of all the Pythons, Michael Palin seems to be the most driven, the most ambitious, the most determined to push himself. It's easy enough to ascribe this to a good, old-fashioned, middle-class ethic, but it seems to go deeper than that. Palin has always maintained a boyish curiosity about life and has always looked to further himself. Not that he sees it quite like that.

> There are still many things I would like to do that I haven't done, and now I can sort of pick and choose, but if it were just up to me, it would be very easy to just sit at home and read books. It all gets slightly shapeless. Throughout my life, I've had people push me into things, which I need, to be committed. Which has turned out to be good – things I might not have done myself. I'm always aware of that. It started at university with Robert Hewison, who pushed me into doing cabaret at Oxford, and I've always had someone like that. Terry Jones is another one. I think there's a certain danger in just sitting there and making all the right moves, so I need to be pushed.

It's hard to believe all that 'I need to be pushed' bit. What Palin has is an extraordinary attitude that says, 'If I do what I enjoy doing – as opposed to what I think will be a good career move – it will all work out.' What seems to drive him much more than money, or the trappings of success, is the creative urge. He genuinely seems to be impelled to do things. Many of us say things like, 'I think I'll try a bit of painting' (or gardening, or flower-arranging), but few of us manage to get round to it. Palin seems to be one of those rare characters who does actually get round to it. Again, we could argue that he's got the freedom of not being burdened by the financial imperative. But that can be a double-edged sword.

After *Python*, after the films, it would be have been very easy for him to keep doing what he knows he can do and what he knows people like. But he didn't. He kept trying new things and for a while in the mid- to late seventies, it seemed he was going through the creative arts, ticking them off one by one. In the end the only thing that held his attention was what had grabbed it as a kid: travel.

Chapter Seven

The Passport Years

'Mike's always wanted to travel. I hadn't quite realized, but in 1970–71 he and I did a little trip to the States because we didn't think *Python* would ever go well in the States and had some time on our hands. Mike said, 'Why don't we do a trip?' so we sat down on my back doorstep and got out an atlas and arbitrarily chose eight destinations in the States and got something called a Discount 50 ticket. There was a deal that if you chose eight destinations you could get 50 per cent off the ticket. So we did this trip around the States. I hadn't quite realized it, but it was Mike's urge to travel. It came from him. I wouldn't have thought of it.'

TERRY JONES

Palin had always been a traveller. Even before he travelled, he was a traveller. His father had travelled but, maybe because of his stammer, maybe because of his nature, he never talked about it. The young Palin had something much better to fire the imagination than anything so rooted in reality.

I was a trainspotter when I was young. I used to stand on the station in Sheffield and look at the train and see these people come in from Edinburgh who were going to London. What sophistication. Sometimes you could see them in the dining car having their dinner and to someone like me who was fairly trapped in his home town, it was just extraordinary. To be conveyed across the country from Scotland's capital to England's capital, whilst having your dinner! I was very excited by it all.

It's so easy to knock trainspotting, but it's amazing how many small-town boys fall for its pleasures: your imagination can go anywhere.

One of the most important days of my life was when I learned to ride a bicycle. Suddenly I was free to travel without my parents. It wasn't very far to start with, but after a while I was covering ten, fifteen, twenty miles. Sheffield was a grimy industrial city, but within an hour you could get out and into absolutely unspoiled, rather wild, desolate, Heathcliff-type, moorland country. Sometimes I would imagine that I was going up to Scotland on a train and I would stop at these various places by the roadside, and they would represent the stations on the way up to Scotland.

Palin's first proper travels came, like most people, when he was a student. A friend had a place in Greece. That sort of thing. When he joined the Pythons he still travelled, but it was a night here, a night there. And then there were days off spent keeping Graham company or recuperating after keeping Graham company.

When there was work to do, he'd take himself off, mostly alone, to write and explore. There was a story he told a journalist about when he started travelling as a Python. In Barcelona, on one of his writing breaks, he went to:

> the sort of place where they give you six glasses and fourteen spoons and practically change the tablecloth between courses. Because I went early and the Spaniards dine very late, I was the only person there. I was terribly embarrassed, the waiters kept bringing out these specialities of the house to show me – huge fish and slabs of meat and finally a lobster. I looked at this lobster and didn't know what to say about it. I knew I didn't want to eat it. Then the waiter said, 'He not deada, he just very colda,' and I was just thinking, oh, I wish the other Pythons were here, this would be a great *Python* sketch, and then the waiter said, 'And how is Brian's life?' and I realized he knew. All this treatment because I was a Python. It was very funny, but a bit of a shock being recognized in Spain.

But you know what they say about travel. The more you do, the more you want to do. The bug never went. As the seventies turned into the eighties and Palin found himself a proper job as a star, with the financial benefits that go with it, he said, 'My one serious ambition is still the same – to be an explorer. I do seriously want to find out what it's like to be eaten alive by a piranha fish.'

Eighty Days

Around the World in Eighty Days took Palin in a completely different direction. East. More importantly, he went from being a multi-skilled, multi-talented, artistic jack of all trades to become one of the most familiar faces in the land. It was also when Palin officially became the nicest man in the world. Before anyone starts getting all precious about the phrase 'jack of all trades' (Jonathan Miller famously once said that he doesn't like being criticized as a jack of all trades by people who are scarcely jacks of one), Michael himself said, 'I rather see myself as that, jack of all trades.'

It all came about in a typically Palin way. Back in 1980, he was approached to do a programme in the BBC 2 series *Great Railways Journeys of the World*. For Palin, this was a blissful job. 'I'd been talking on the radio about my favourite form of transport, which happened to be the train, and the next morning I got a call from the series director.' A blissful job for Palin; baffling for most other people. 'I remember Denis O'Brien of Handmade Films, who was sort of our Python manager for a while, could not believe that I wanted to do a thing on railways when I could have had any film I wanted.'

While everyone else chose to go somewhere exotic for their journey, Michael chose to go from his home in north London to the Kyle of Lochalsh in Scotland.

> I thought, a railway journey through England and Scotland not only will be beautiful, lovely scenery and all, but I get to ride on one of the old steam engines – something I've always wanted to do, something I'd have given my right arm to do twenty years earlier, so I thought, 'Why not now?' I didn't think about whether I should be doing it for career reasons or money reasons or any other reasons. I just thought it would be a good thing to do and a great experience, which is rather the way I approached *Eighty Days* in the end.

In the Palin CV, that programme is strictly second division, but it was perhaps as pivotal as meeting Robert Hewison or Terry Jones. And there was something else interesting about that *Great Railway Journeys* programme. Somewhere in deepest Cornwall, a BBC producer called Clem Vallance happened to be watching.

Around the World with Mr Blobby

'. . . and after the *Nine o'Clock News*, the first in a new series – *Around the World in Eighty Days* with Noel Edmonds.' It does seem an odd idea to take on board, but if the bosses at the BBC had had their way back in 1988, it wouldn't have been Michael Palin at all, but Noel and Mr Blobby crossing the Indian Ocean. A five-man BBC crew, Noel and The Blobster on a dhow. Not that even Edmonds was their first choice.

'The BBC will take great credit for all this,' says Roger Mills, 'but it was all down to Clem Vallance [the series producer and, coincidentally, a Footlight contemporary of Eric Idle]. He came up with this idea – it was a scenario just waiting to be done – and at that time at the BBC the conditioned reflex when it was a travel series was "Send for Alan Whicker."' What did it matter that Whicker was semi-retired and living a happy, comfortable life in Jersey? The feeling, it seems, wasn't so much that Palin wasn't a big enough star but that he wasn't a big enough BBC star. Mills recalls his thinking at the time:

> Michael Palin, to my mind, was part of *Monty Python,* of which, I suppose, John Cleese was the one who predominated. He stuck out, the other Pythons merged in a general mass. But *Python* had stopped ages ago. Michael had been in feature films which generally weren't big Hollywood blockbusters, but they were successful British films. But Clem always wanted Michael. I later found out that he'd seen Michael do a programme about a railway journey . . .
>
> We didn't want Alan Whicker to do it, but it was all sorted out that he was going to do it. So they [the BBC hierarchy] arranged a dinner and Whicker duly arrived. I'd worked with Alan Whicker. We did *Whicker's World* together in Australia. Alan was getting on by then, seventy, something like that.

Fortunately, Vallance and Mills had a cunning plan. They knew what to do and played it perfectly.

> We didn't want Alan and I remember Clem ringing me up and saying, 'What are we going to do?' So I said, 'Well, stress the discomfort of it all,' and at this famous lunch in a pizza restaurant in Shepherd's Bush, Clem came up with the immortal sentence, 'Alan, you'll have to share with the crew when we cross the Indian Ocean in the dhow.' Dead silence. There was a little pebble in the pond and the ripple came to the shore. Alan didn't take much notice after that, he just looked into the middle distance. On the way back to the BBC, one of the executives said to me, 'I think we've got him,' but I knew. A letter came by return, wishing us well and saying that due to the speed with which it would have to be done, just eighty days, he felt he wouldn't have time to prepare his interviews enough.

Was it true, or were they winding Whicker up a bit?

> No, it was absolutely true. In *Eighty Days* there was a dhow and everyone shared. Anyway, that wasn't the end of the story, because the BBC then

Around the World in Eighty Days – *Palin enjoys his first hookah, in Jeddah, Saudi Arabia*

wanted Noel Edmonds and then they wanted the writer Miles Kington [who had written comedy with Jones at Oxford]. He'd just done a good programme about Burma, but his wife was heavily pregnant with their first child and he didn't want to leave her. I don't know why the creator of Mr Blobby didn't do it. Perhaps he was busy with Mr Blobby. The fourth choice was Michael.

Now, of course, it's difficult to imagine anyone else doing it. Maybe Kington, who, judging by his newspaper columns, would seem to be cut from the same cloth as Palin. But Noel Edmonds? What were they thinking of?

One of the advantages Palin had was that although he was a star, he was not so big that he dominated the programme. *A Fish Called Wanda* had not long been out and while it was a popular film, it was not yet a phenomenon. Pre-travel, Palin was still an ex-Python. It seems inconceivable now, in the light of the success of his travel shows, that back then he was considered too small to carry them. 'They didn't think he was a big enough name to make audiences automatically turn on,' says Mills, 'but he was an immediate hit. He was one of these comets in the firmament.'

Eighty Days was something I took on because the timing was right. We had been through the *Python* stage; we'd made a television series and made the movies. I'd done a series of movies culminating in *A Fish Called Wanda* and felt I'd done enough standing around waiting to be called from my caravan. Someone suddenly rang up and said that *Around the World in Eighty Days* was around, would I run with it? And of course, I said I would, because I love travel so much. There's something about travelling when you're doing promotions, like I've done for most of my life, which actually negates any experience. You tend to stay in the same hotels; you see airports, interiors of press conferences, television studios, and that's that. If you really want to see the world, you have to stop for a little bit and say, 'For two or three weeks, I'm going off to wherever.' And although I knew it was what I wanted to do, I'd never had room for that in my life at all. So along comes a chance to travel around the world, and get paid for it, and have it be part of my work, so it took care of a whole lot of different problems all at one go.

It was also perfect because it wasn't so much an experiment as something the BBC expected nothing from. A nice programme maybe, but nothing in particular. A bit like one of those *Great Railway Journeys*, but on a bigger budget. However, life never works out quite like you expect and there were two things that turned this potentially nice travelogue into something much more than either the BBC or the team behind it expected.

From the moment *Eighty Days* started, you knew that there was something perfect going on. Palin, it quickly became obvious, had a rare gift for communication. He could get – physically and emotionally – where the viewer wanted him to get. This was a completely different character from the one we'd previously seen. Palin pulled off the rare trick of being very professional but very warm and human.

'He used to write in his passport "actor" and maybe that's the way he sees himself. Maybe he was acting the part of being a travel presenter, but anyway he fell into the role – if he saw it as a role – very naturally,' says Mills. It had long been apparent that Palin was a very good actor – by far the best actor of the Pythons. 'He's the only real actor among us,' said Terry Gilliam. 'The rest of us are just caricaturists.' And while 'revolutionary' isn't necessarily a word you'd readily associate with Michael Palin, he took a new approach to the business of presenting a television show.

He very unselfishly did something that Whicker would never do. He brought the crew into it and made people realize it wasn't just him. There was an infrastructure, there were forty pieces of baggage that had to be lugged around. He wasn't afraid to talk about things like lavatories. He would address the camera. He would address the cameraman behind the camera, and while this is now commonplace, it wasn't commonplace then. It was really very new. Palin himself just puts it down to basic enjoyment.

> I just enjoy learning from other people. I have no real qualifications other than a history degree from Oxford. I am not particularly good at anything. I am not particularly practical. I am not particularly good at languages. What I am quite good at is getting people to trust me fairly quickly. I don't say, 'You've got to fit in with the way I am.' I just try and say, 'Look, tell me what's going on here.' Another very important ingredient in travel is to be able to be aware of how ridiculous you may seem to people sometimes. You also have got to have a sense of wonder, which I think I probably do have. I am not a great cook, I am not a great artist, but I love art and I love food, so I am the perfect traveller – always on the cultural scrounge.

It's all very well loving art and loving food, but when that food happens to be deep-fried snake's balls in eyeball juice . . .

> I feel that food is so much a part of a local culture, and if you're going to try to understand and communicate with people whose language you don't speak very much, you have to be able to eat their food and drink their drink, because that's often the way they show their hospitality. I just hope I'm not going to have something that's truly foul and awful.

Sometimes hope just isn't enough.

I've been reasonably lucky. I've had low-grade bugs, but I came across some very odd things, including maggots in guacamole sauce in a restaurant in Mexico City, actually on the menu, and a wonderful palm wine that was served to me in an Indian village in the Amazon. It's very, very strong, and in the parts of the Amazon where there's plenty of sugar growing, they ferment it with the sugar, and if they don't have sugar in the area, then the old ladies spit in it and ferment it with their saliva. I'd had a couple of swigs of it, so I asked my guide very nervously, 'Is there much sugar growing in this village?' And he shook his head and said, 'No. No sugar around here.' And I thought, 'I'll survive that.' But you do get sick. Your bowels seem to lurk in wait for you until you get to the most wretched and miserable lavatory facilities in the world, and then they start letting you down.

During *Eighty Days*, one scene caused a particular fuss back home, if not in Palin's bowels. In Kwangchow, China, a live snake was beheaded and disembowelled for his meal. All done in front of the camera – the skinning, the placing of the snake's head, warm tongue still flicking, on the plate next to a saucer which contained the snake's gall bladder. The Reptile Protection Trust made a complaint which the Broadcasting Standards Council upheld. Palin, for his part, found the meal quite tasty.

Why not? It's a way of life. It happens. I was criticized when I featured cock-fighting in the Philippines in *Full Circle*, but it happens. You can't change the world by using different words. It's a rule of travel that it's a good idea to eat what the locals eat. I've probably eaten a bit of dog and cat in China. To them, they're not pets, just the food that there's most of.

As any traveller knows, the 'it's a way of life, it happens' philosophy helps when you're away.

Here we live the life of consumer excess, when we strive to buy a better car, yet in the Amazon a tin roof is considered a luxury, or in Africa, where they walk four miles to fetch water for the day. Of course there's an imbalance in the way they live and we live, but sometimes it's the simplest things that change people's lives. I've seen how just a few hundred quid can create low-technology solutions, like building a well in a village so the women don't have to face an eight-mile journey every day. By the way, it's always the women – the men just lie around smoking and drinking.

According to Mills, Palin's only ever refused to do one thing,

> and that wasn't on one of the travel series. I once did a little series with him
> called *Palin's Column*, where he was on the Isle of Wight and he was doing
> a column for the *Isle of Wight County Press*. There was going to be a scene
> where he's chatting with the editor. The editor's a big golf man, but Michael
> refused point blank. He was not going to play golf. He'd do anything else but
> he wouldn't play golf.

Maybe he can't play?

'Well, you could say that about anything. Can he ride a camel? There are lots of
things he's done that he can't really do but he was prepared to have a go at, but
not golf.'

So there you go. Michael Palin's happy to eat deep-fried snake's balls, but getting
out a four iron . . . Absolutely not. You've got to draw the line somewhere.

If you watch *Eighty Days* now, it seems obvious that at the beginning they were
searching for a style. Palin ran around doing loads of interviews, talking to people,
getting advice and not doing an awful lot of travelling. 'I think the talk at the beginning of *Eighty Days* held it up,' says Mills.

> We wouldn't do that now. Sitting down and talking to people, I don't think
> that's his forte at all; he's not a journalist, he hasn't come up through News,
> but he has got a lot better at doing interviews. To begin with, he wasn't that
> good. It was actually quite hard to edit. That wasn't his fault, it just wasn't
> his training. He has got a lot better, but then so has everyone else in the team.

Palin was hard to edit because he didn't interview people, he talked to them. They
didn't answer him, they talked to him.

The other thing that *Eighty Days* had going for it was the inbuilt race against
time. 'They didn't have to know the story, but they did know that it was a story,
so you don't have to do very much setting up at all. I could use Fogg's name so the
fictional hero goes ahead of me and provides me with a drama,' says Palin now.

> The BBC sent us off, hoping it would be a success, with, I think, no great
> expectations. When we got back in seventy-nine days and eight hours, we felt
> we had a success, and a rather good story, because it didn't look as if we
> would do it – going through the Arabian peninsula, Saudi Arabia and through
> Dubai, across the Indian Ocean to India. Going across India to Madras, we
> fell catastrophically behind, we thought we're never going to do this.

That's a bit too good to be true, isn't it? Seventy-nine days and eight hours? Was there an element of deliberately cutting it fine?

> No, but I remember the cameraman – and by this stage we knew we were going to do it – he got very blasé. We were in Le Havre and just poised to get back, we were on a container ship going up to Felixstowe and he said, 'Why don't we make it a bit more difficult for ourselves and get in with maybe just an hour to spare? We can get the ferry from Le Havre to Portsmouth, and then get the railway up from Portsmouth to Waterloo.'

Going so far and trusting things to British Rail? What sort of madness is that? Fortunately, Mills knew a bit about the state of the railways in the UK. 'I said that having come so far and having gone through so much, I'm not going to dice with death, because if anything went wrong I would never forgive myself.' Had the *Eighty Days* team taken that cameraman's advice, it could have been much worse than simply not making Fogg's deadline. 'You know, that was the day of the Clapham rail disaster and if we had done that, if we had taken that train, we would not have been on the train that crashed, but we would not have got through Clapham Junction.' And lost? 'And lost.'

> People said, 'Oh, you cheated, didn't you? Didn't you? You flew a bit, didn't you? Oh, come on. It's too good to be true.' But no, we didn't cheat at all. We travelled every inch of that route.

A nice postscript to this is that the radio disc jockey Simon Bates thought if Palin could do it, he could do better. 'Simon Bates tried to copy it and he did it on sound radio, only he went the other way. We went east, he started by going west, and he went across the Atlantic and he was days ahead, but we said, "You wait till he gets to Arabia." And of course, he did and he failed, he had to get an aircraft.'

Coming back from a travel venture is always likely to cause a bit of depression, but for the *Eighty Days* crew the homecoming experience was particularly grim, as Palin explains, 'We made it back to London only to find ourselves on the underground with a bomb warning going off. We were two miles from our goal and I thought, "This is the end".' It wasn't. They made it through to the Reform Club, who welcomed them with . . . closed doors. 'They wouldn't let us in to film. I had a feeling of absolute frustration at their helpfulness.' He probably didn't have the right tie. But

---

On the Isle of Wight, the location for Palin's Column

there was a glorious irony. They could go round the world and speak the same language as everyone they met. They could laugh in Lisbon, chat in China, talk in Timbuktu. They could eat shredded snake with broccoli and deep-fried balls. But could they get past the class barrier in England? No.

Palin was the first person to do a travel show without making it either some glossy Whickeresque fantasy-island deal – all aspiration and greed – or a *Wish You Were Here* holiday programme.

> I am a big fan of Whicker, I think he's brilliant, although he's taken a path quite different from mine. His technique as a reporter is great, but I can't do that. I just kept getting the feeling that this was just a huge exercise in self-indulgence, a bit like *Python*. I knew I was going to enjoy it and I knew that the crew were going to enjoy it, but the viewers? I was worried that we needed more analysis and we'd go to all these wonderful places only for people to say, 'Yeah, great. But what have we actually found out?' At the end, I thought, if I can respond as genuinely and honestly as possible to what's going on, then we've got the basis of the programme.

That was the key: the idea that Palin was genuine and honest. People empathized with him. He wasn't an expert, he didn't speak twelve languages and know the names of all the trees and the stories behind all the temples and everything – but he'd ask. It sounds obvious and simple, and like all the best ideas it *is* obvious and simple – but it hadn't been done before. It also helped that Palin was able to reveal yet another string to his bow: he was an extraordinarily gifted communicator. He could just be himself and we'd be there with him, that nice Michael Palin. He wasn't an expert. He wasn't even a comic genius. He was one of us.

> My approach was to play it naturally, which I prefer. I don't like doing a presentation. I don't like having to have my hair brushed a certain way and my suit put on and . . . whatever, the way presenters appear to be. I would rather be myself, and when I travel, I'm not consciously any different from the way I am at home.

There was a key moment when it all became clear.

> Our editor was looking at a shot in Bombay. It was originally down as a ten-minute piece, but then he said, 'It's really nice, some of these relationships Michael has with the crew there, he can't hurry it.' So the director said they'd

let me work on it and we came out with a fifty-minute piece all based on the dhow. We looked at it and thought, that's ridiculous. But then we thought, well, actually it does develop in rather a nice way. Because of the circumstances, I had to rely, for my life, almost literally, on a group of Gujaratis who don't speak English. Then I thought, looking at it, that's what makes it a very different kind of programme. So we put it in and said to the BBC, you've commissioned us for six but we've actually got seven.

That same programme – the one with the dhow – was also the one that finally won the critics over.

The first programme had received some pretty cutting reviews, which said things like, 'Oh yes, Michael Palin going on a trip, but he's not the proper documentary type.' But the third episode – which was that dhow programme – turned it around. I remember the critic in the *Independent*, Mark Lawson, who had been quite critical, actually re-reviewed it and said, 'I've got this wrong. It's actually quite interesting and we're seeing something that we haven't seen anywhere else.' It was nice that people took the trouble to have another look. At the same time, the morning after that third programme had gone out, the BBC finally got the book published. They didn't get it out in time. I was supposed to go to a specialist travel shop in Covent Garden called Stanfords for a 12.30 signing. The phone rang, a PR woman from the BBC said she'd had a message from the shop and they'd asked if I could get there a bit earlier because they'd got a lot of requests after last night's show. So I got there at about 9.30, went in and they just didn't know what was happening. Orders were coming in, more books were coming in from the BBC, being trolleyed around. It was just wonderful. There were people who were being turned away and told to come back in the afternoon, so we were signing books long after lunch as well. So, that was the moment, that was the moment I realized we'd hit some sort of goal in this thing. There was an audience out there, and the audience figures held steady and began to grow.

Was it disorientating, this sudden rush of popularity?

No, not at all. Actually it was a terrific feeling. *Python* was something that had became popular over a fairly long period of time and so we'd grown into it and I'd never really had a popular hit with anything I'd done. But this was really exhilarating. It was fantastic.

Second Only to Noddy

Eighty Days took Palin on to another new level. It introduced him to a different kind of stardom. He went from being a famous person to being a fixture. He'd taken that leap to become the sort of person the BBC had hoped would front *Eighty Days* in the first place. After the success of the book of the series, the word was that Palin's royalty cheques were so large, they had to be personally countersigned by the Director General of the BBC – 'The BBC said I was second only to Noddy in world sales,' said a self-deprecatory Palin. It wasn't only Palin who was celebrating – it was a case of 'trebles all round' for those executives who had initially opposed signing Palin.

Given his track record, it would have been no surprise if at this juncture Palin had decided against doing another travelogue and gone off instead and done something completely out of character, like writing a novel about a postal worker who's obsessed with Ernest Hemingway, for example. But he stayed with the travel. After *Eighty Days,* he took a short break in which he didn't do much – wrote and starred in a feature film (*American Friends*, 1990), took a straight acting role in an Alan Bleasdale television drama (*GBH*, 1991) and did a voice-over for a children's video (*Jack and the Beanstalk*, 1991) – before he signed on the dotted line for another travel series.

Palin in American Friends

If he'd been having second thoughts about the wisdom of his decision, his experience on *American Friends* would have sorted that out. *American Friends* was a project particularly close to Palin's heart and its relative failure probably hurt him more than anything else in his professional life. It's a delightful film made all the more delightful because it tells the true story of Palin's great-grandfather, the Reverend Edward Palin. A distant relative from the West Country contacted him about a box of family effects that they'd found. Did Michael want to take possession? Palin and his sister, Angela, drove down to Cirencester to collect a musty box full of old photos in even older frames, ledgers, account books and notebooks. Palin tried to work his way through the notebooks to find out more about this character who had written so copiously 120 years earlier, but it was hard going. He put it all away. Picked it up a few years later. Put it away again. Kept being drawn to it, the idea of his great-grandfather, but couldn't find anything that really gripped him. 'I persevered and almost at the end of the diary found the moment when Edward Palin stumbled upon the young Brita. Stumbled and fell.' That was it. That was what the romantic inside Palin had hoped to find.

Edward Palin, it transpired, was a brilliant divinity don, the vice-president of St John's College, Oxford. He had it all in front of him, but then, on holiday in the Swiss Alps, he met Brita. And that was that. When he returned to Oxford, he tried to get the college authorities to waive the rule stating that dons must be bachelors, but they wouldn't. He left Oxford, they went to Paris to get married and then returned to live and practise in Linton, Hertfordshire, where Edward was the vicar. When Palin casually mentioned the story to Eric Idle, Idle said that he must make it into a film.

Palin starred in and co-wrote *American Friends* (with producer Tristan Powell, who'd directed *East of Ipswich* and *Number 27*), but it was not well received. There are no laughs. *American Friends* was a nice film – looked lovely and was as charming as could be. Perhaps it lacked something hard in its soul, but that's true of Palin too.

It was my baby, in a sense, but I still saw it as a team film and I wasn't too precious about it. The problem was that no one really had the chance to see it and make up their minds. It had taken about three or four years to get together, and in the end we produced a really high-quality, good-looking, quite touching story. But it was sunk by distribution problems – people in charge of distribution who really didn't understand it. It was sunk in the US, where it had to be treated quite carefully because it was an art-house movie. It was sunk by one review in the *New York Times* which was quite savage, again one of those reviews where you think, this is not about the film, this is about the guy. Someone coming along who's having a very, very unpleasant day and is forced to see this film, and I thought, this is ridiculous. All this work's been put in and it's a lovely film. I was very proud of it and I thought, what's the point?

Is there a parallel with the fate of *Fierce Creatures*?

With *American Friends* I honestly think it was a case of a really nice film just not getting seen. With *Fierce Creatures*, I think it was the film itself that could have been stronger. But the combination of the two of those . . . I realized, however hard you work on a film, someone out there who is responsible for showing it and getting it seen can ruin it for you and destroy it.

Those two films soured me slightly about the way films are treated, but then *Pole to Pole*, which I made shortly after *American Friends*, was just as successful as *Eighty Days*. We didn't have the story behind us, but we had Michael Palin going from pole to pole, and that seemed to hold an audience. That was very surprising and revealing, and crucial to the decision I had to make at that time, whether to go back to acting in films or do more of this travelling.

'Let's Go Down'

It was partly because of the response to *American Friends*, but more because *Eighty Days* was so popular that Palin was inspired to do another trip. And all that positive feedback about something that – despite his generosity in crediting his film crews – is your show must be very hard to resist.

When we did a programme like the dhow, it obviously struck a chord. A lot of people said that I made them feel as though they were on the journey with me, and they were very close to it all and it made them want to travel to the same areas. Also, and this is perhaps the nicest thing of all, I heard from some teachers in the States that they show their kids our programmes because they're not patronizing and don't talk down and we don't try to suggest that we're better than anyone else. That's high praise, and I'm very flattered people should think that.

There is something about travel – you finish a journey and think, that's it, but then you realize you've really only just started. '*Eighty Days* didn't cure me of the travel bug. Just the opposite in fact – it stimulated me and made me more curious about what lies out there.'

As friendly headmaster in Alan Bleasdale's GBH

Pole to Pole came about because, as Clem Vallance said, 'We've done across. Let's go down.' It was a wonderful trip – five and a half months, 12,500 miles, seventeen countries. To a travel junkie, things don't get much better.

> I thought we ought to have a go at another one, partly to satisfy my own curiosity and partly because of the very different route, down through Finland and Russia and right through Africa – from Cairo to the Cape, the historic route down the Nile. We knew we couldn't emulate the *Eighty Days* format, because part of the fun of it was that it was a race against time, and I don't think you can do a proper travel series like that, with three days' break in eighty days of filming. Physically, it's almost impossible. Looking back, in *Eighty Days* I was quite surprised that we got as much out of it as we did in the end. *Eighty Days* was an unknown quantity. I just didn't know what it was going to be, how it was going to be, what tone we'd adopt, how it would work. In the end, the people we met made the show – it just wrote

itself as we went round. This one isn't quite so unknown. The technique we now know. Roughly the sort of tone of it, we know. So it's really just the places we go through that are going to be different – but they're very different and there's less time for luxury. A lot of it will be much rougher.

There was a different pressure on Palin during *Pole to Pole*. When they'd filmed *Eighty Days*, no one was expecting anything. It became a hit series after the event. But when they set off to film *Pole to Pole*, things had changed and they were now the BBC's golden boys.

'*Pole to Pole* was, I think, the pressure one. There wasn't the time pressure there had been in *Eighty Days*, but that was part of the story then, that's what made it exciting. It was an experiment. We went into it joyfully and happily and if we failed, we failed,' says Roger Mills. 'Also we had to water down our principles. Our principle on *Eighty Days* was that this would be real travel in real time on the surface of the globe. Now, you had to take aeroplanes.'

Pole to Pole – aboard the Nile Valley Express

They had an idea that would have got the series off to a fantastic start and would have solved the plane problem. 'We were going to begin *Pole to Pole* with Michael at the North Pole,' says Mills.

A submarine comes through the ice, Michael gets on it and travels down to Norway by nuclear submarine. If we'd have done that, we wouldn't have needed to take any aeroplanes. The Royal Navy would have cooperated, but you needed an Awacs aircraft above you to get you into the right position and the Brits didn't have one. The Americans did, but they said, look, in fact it's a tactical secret where our nuclear subs are and we can't tell you at this time where they'll be. It probably won't be the North Pole. Do you mind doing it in Canada or Alaska? We thought, well, it would be a fantastic shot but it wouldn't be the North Pole. The argument flew back and forward. Some people said, 'Ice looks like ice, doesn't it?' and the argument raged on, but in the end we thought, no, it's got to be the North Pole, even if it means flying, and we had to fly. You see, we couldn't cheat.

The other thing was, we set off from northern Canada and the pilot would only go if it was clear sky because the wind blows up hard chunks of ice on the pole and he wants to see from the shadows cast by the sun how tall they are, because he can't do it any other way. But when we came in to land, there was thick cloud cover, he didn't have his shadows and that was really hair-raising. We were going round and round and round, using up precious fuel and in the end we just had to land, we just had to make a decision. And we would come in low and have to abort, and this went on and on. In the end, he said, 'Sorry, folks. We've got to come down here.' And we're all praying, because we thought that this could really be extremely nasty. Anyway, the result of all this flying around meant we did not land at the North Pole.

Not that it would ever have been straightforward.

Where the actual North Pole is, I don't know, because there's the magnetic pole, there's the real pole and there's another pole, but our compass was reading 89 degrees, 59 minutes and 59 seconds, so we were a second off the true measurement of 90 degrees north. It was a great shame, because it would have been an absolutely fantastic beginning to the series.

When we landed, we had to keep one engine running, because if that had gone, we wouldn't have been able to take off. We had enough fuel, I think, to be down about twenty minutes on the pole. It was a very, very short time.

Just enough for Michael to get down, do his thing with his pole, do a piece to camera, do a trail for later on, take a team photograph, have a pee at the pole and then take off.

You don't want to be fluffing your lines in those circumstances.

'The other thing that struck me was the open water at the pole. I thought it would just be a load of ice, but it's not and that presented another problem with the landing because the ice is moving and is constantly freezing over.' Somewhere that looks solid suddenly isn't. And when you haven't got much fuel and you can't see those vital shadows . . . 'You don't think about it at the time, but afterwards you think, that was dodgy, wasn't it?'

Pole to Pole was filmed in 1991, which was an interesting year. 'We started it all . . . I think we finally precipitated the total collapse of the Soviet Union. Within two days of leaving Odessa in the Soviet Union, the generals' coup happened and the whole thing fell apart,' said Palin. 'We talked to people from Ukraine and Estonia who said, "Well, maybe in thirty years' time we'll get our independence." By Christmas, they'd got it.'

Largely, the trip went well.

We travelled overland and didn't catch any major diseases – though I did crack a rib white-water-rafting on the Zambesi. Apart from that, there were no great problems as far as I was concerned. Some of the crew got sick, but we managed to film every day despite the extremes of heat and cold.

During the journey, he encountered the worst place he's ever slept.

It was a hotel in Ethiopia . . . Well, hotel would actually probably be an exaggeration, but it was called a hotel, and it turned out to be a sort of mud hut with a clay floor, and the pillow was made of old sacks. Whenever I turned my torch on to look what time it was, about a dozen insects of the cockroach variety scuttled away. I've never had a night when I've been more in fear of being infested, or whatever. At the same time, there were all sorts of amorous noises going on just beyond the bamboo clay partition, and I thought, how can they do it with these bugs all over the place? Never again.

Was it worse than the dhow in *Eighty Days*? 'No, the dhow was fine, because we slept out on the deck, under the stars, with a cool breeze as the ship moved down the Persian Gulf. That was great. It was bad to shit on, but it was great to sleep on.'
  And the worst/best form of transport?

Probably the dog-sledge. It's a very bizarre thing, being tugged along. You don't realize it when you see them gliding through the snow, but they have to evacuate their bowels whilst on the move, so there's a constant smell as you go along, which rather detracted from the romance of it all. The particular team I went with were just like a group of high-spirited kids. There was a moment where we had to stop because there was a huge fall of snow and after spending ages getting them all to lie down, the guide went off to find a way over this snow ridge, leaving me sitting there. Then one of the dogs got up to scratch his ear. Immediately another got up and then another and then suddenly they were off, taking me up over this ridge and down the other side while the guide screamed at them. It was quite funny, really.

Palin being Palin, they couldn't get out without a least one surreal turn.

We were airlifted from the southern part of Chile to the central part of the Antarctic plateau, looked after on the small base there and then flown to the pole. When we got to the pole, there was a big American base there called the Scott/Amundsen Base, with a sort of hamburger joint underneath the pole, and it was rather like going to a *Python* fan convention. The most remote part of the Earth and there were people there with copies of *Wanda* that they want you to sign. That didn't happen to Captain Scott.

The Best Job in the World

One of the interesting things about Palin's career has been the way that it shadows the stages of man. It started off with him learning how to do the things that he wanted to do. Then, in his twenties, during the *Python* era, he was all spiky and questioning, sarcastic and cynical, his energy directed, if not towards the overthrow of society, then towards questioning the status quo, mocking the sacred cows that prop up the establishment. As life got more comfortable and settled, he calmed down, becoming more content with what's what. What does it tell us that while he found popularity and respect in his younger spiky years, it was only later, when he settled for warmth, that he found mass appeal. Was there any sense of frustration that he did all this cutting-edge stuff and yet it's the Mr Nice Guy persona that's touched the soul of the nation?

No, no. It doesn't worry me at all. I don't see a huge difference between what I was doing in *Python* and what I'm doing now. The good thing about *Python* was a lot of it was stuff you can do when you're young, well, younger. You can question everything, you can be more outrageous and in a sense *Python* was a lot of negatives. It was saying, 'We don't like this. We don't like that. We're going to have a go at this. We don't like the way conventional programmes are made.' And that can carry you so far, but after a bit you get rather tired of the negative side. I've never been very interested in that. I've always wanted to be more positive in the things that I do and I see the travel programmes as being very positive. Also, I don't see them as being soft. If I felt, well, I'm just doing a holiday programme . . . Mr Nice Guy introducing all these various holiday resorts, telling you about all these nice places to go to, then I would feel that I'd taken a very wrong turn.

But I regard the travel programmes as being quite as cutting-edge in a sense as *Python* was. Not particularly for their technique, not even in their attitudes, but in the way that we make them. There aren't any programmes quite like that – and I've only just realized this, because of people's reaction to them. You can have people like Ranulph Fiennes or Benedict Allen, who do incredibly difficult physical things, take camels across the Namibian desert, go across the ice, all that sort of thing. At the same time, you can have very good storytellers and academics like Michael Wood and David Attenborough, but I do something which is different from all that, and which makes me feel I'm still doing something which is quite different from the norm, still in the spirit of *Python*, something that's quite hard to define.

I think I provide programmes which lead people to see themselves through me and realize that everyone makes mistakes, that you goof things up, that you should have learned the language better, that you get ill if you eat certain foods and, if you really like it . . . you can go off and do it for yourself. I've not attempted to pre-empt what anyone else has tried to do – so it's got that pleasure of seeing inadequacy and incompetence at the same time as you see achievement and elation and the wonders of the world.

Is it the best job in the world?

Most days, yes, but it's still . . . it's a long time away. Don't forget, you're not just travelling, having a good time. You're providing programmes, you have to deliver material. Every day, apart from the odd rest day, you have to bring something back – very often you'll be in an extraordinary place for a very short time and you'll have to capture that because the schedules are quite tight and often you either capture it or you miss it. You have to work hard and that's what I quite like about it, to be honest. It's like a small commando team: everyone has to know their job, everyone has to be superb at their job.

The other thing is just one's own attitude, and I'm aware that I'm out there spending a whole lot of the BBC's money, with a reputation back home and . . . am I going to be up to it? You think about that every morning, you know. Maybe you had a bad night, something like that, you're tired, you're ill, you have to go out there and somehow deal with it and make it interesting. You can never ever assume that whatever you do, people are going to watch it. Each day, you have to be aware of what you're doing, which is communicating what's going on to an audience, and that's really quite hard to do. You've got to tread the line between whingeing about how awful it is and getting on with the beauty of it. Somehow, you've got to tread that middle ground – you can't whinge about yourself. Well, you can, but it's dangerous because in the end people will turn round and say, 'Lucky bastard. He's got the best job in the world.' The great thing about the programmes, the thing that makes it safer for me, is that if I'm feeling rotten, people love that. If I get it wrong, people love that more.

One of the things I think is that I can look back on all my work and say, 'Well, that's an achievement.' We had an audience of, I think, 9.5 million for a journey across the Sudan – a sand desert refugee camp, muddy roads, slow progress, and people stayed with it. If you'd put a programme in the schedule saying that, you'd be lucky if you got half a million, so that's why I do it.

Chapter Eight

The Last of the Big Journeys

After finishing *Pole to Pole*, Michael Palin said, 'Well, I know I'll always want to travel, but this is going to be the last of the really big journeys that we do.'

Clem Vallance and Roger Mills said, 'Yeah. So when do you want to go?'

Travel plus television has two in-built problems. First, if you're going to do another travelogue, it's really got to be bigger and better than the one you did before. Second, where are you going to go? The world's not that big a place. It had been mooted to do a trip round the Equator and, in theory, it's a cool idea, but the reality is that the viewer is going to be looking at a lot of water. What was the answer?

> After *Around the World in Eighty Days* and *Pole to Pole*, the question I was most often asked was, 'Is there anywhere you haven't been?' As soon as I started getting out my Pacific maps, it became clear that there were lots of places, and that a journey round the Pacific Rim would cover a great many of them, and shed light on a huge part of the world I knew embarrassingly little about. A circle may sound like a neat, controllable entity, like a hubcap or the face of Big Ben, but when its diameter is 11,000 miles, it takes on epic proportions. And *Full Circle* indeed proved to be an epic.

That was from Palin's introduction to *Full Circle*, the book of the series. As for the Pacific Rim, 'People confidently talk about it as an entity, as the new sort of powerhouse of the world, but what exactly is it?' The trip took in just about every type of terrain there is, just about every type of climate, every shade of life. They travelled around 50,000 miles and were on the road for 270 days, 'returning home briefly to do some laundry and save our marriages'.

He's got the whole world in his hand . . .

Full Circle was the biggest, most difficult and most ambitious of Palin's travel shows to date. Starting off on Little Diomede Island, a tiny rock in Alaska's Bering Strait, the most north-westerly point in the United States, going down the east coast of Russia, Japan, China, the Philippines, Indonesia, Australia, New Zealand, across to the southern tip of Chile, up the west coast of South America, through central America, up the west coast of North America, across Canada, through Alaska and back across the Bering Sea. Remote locations perhaps, but they were expecting him.

> Right at the beginning, on the island of Diomede, I'm rhapsodizing about this bleak island on the International Date Line, on the Arctic Circle, this treeless place, inhabited by a few Eskimos catching whales and seals during the winter season, and as we left on our whaleskin boat, this little group of Eskimos shuffled up to me. I thought it was going to be a sincere Eskimo farewell or something, but one of them pointed at me and said, 'Aren't you the guy from *Monty Python and the Holy Grail?*'

Eric Idle suggested that they call the series *Palin's Rim*, but curiously the BBC didn't go for it. That didn't stop the *Independent* newspaper buying the suggestion and – in full seriousness – running articles referring to it by that name. In a way, it wasn't such an idle suggestion. One of the things that Palin has taken to chatting about is that whole toilet issue. Travellers – give them half an hour in India and they're off talking about bowels and stuff. Wittingly or not, Palin has tapped into this brilliantly and now it's almost as if his toilet habits are a matter of national concern.

It was the biggest series you've done, wasn't it?

> It is the biggest and I think the best, as far as I'm concerned, certainly. It's the one I've got the most out of, the richest and the most varied, with the greatest number of different countries and the greatest number of different things seen, so in that sense it's the most pleasurable. But it's also been the toughest. It's hard to go out travelling and experience it all the way around. On certain days, and for weeks at a time, sometimes there's no respite, no really comfortable place we can stop and say, 'OK, well, that's just the day. Tonight we'll be in a five-star hotel.' It just doesn't happen. I think, considering the territory we went through, we were lucky not to get very sick. We were lucky not to have any accidents, and I think we've had our fair share of good fortune.

It's not as if filming *Full Circle* wasn't demanding enough. It's not as if being away for 270 days (not including laundry breaks) and travelling 50,000 miles wasn't gruelling enough. There was also some unfinished business that Palin had to take care of.

I was filming *Fierce Creatures* with John Cleese during the summer that preceded our journey and, as movies tend to do, the movie overran by about two and a half weeks, so I was still stuck in that closet with John Cleese and a spider and Carey Lowell and all of us in various stages of undress three days before I was due to leave for Alaska.

And . . . you know how sometimes, if you've been working really hard and then you stop, your body just . . . shuts down for a while. You get a cold, if you're lucky, and if you're not, you get laid up. Well, you get laid up if you've got the chance to lay. If you're on a slow boat to Alaska, it's a different matter. I did get a really bad cold, which I think sometimes comes after you've done a very concentrated spell of hard work, and I really did feel at the very beginning of the journey that we wouldn't make it through the first episode, let alone the rest. But you sort of keep going; you get this mental attitude which keeps you going in the end.

It was during the filming of *Full Circle* that Palin felt the most frightened he's ever been on his travels.

We were going through a pretty rough area of downtown Bogotá, in Colombia, an extraordinary city where great wealth and numbing poverty go hand in hand. It's also a place where a lot of drug trafficking goes on, and we went down to this area called Bullet Street, which I suppose might be seen as asking for trouble. We were told never to get out of the car and to keep the camera down as much as possible. But somebody caught sight of the camera, and these guys peered from the cardboard huts where they lived, and threw concrete blocks and bits of wood and whatever they could at the car. We made off pretty quickly.

Surely they were lucky the locals didn't take the name of the street seriously.

No, there were no bullets. At the end of it, our cameraman asked if he could go back again so he could get some better shots. Our guide said, 'Don't be ridiculous. Next time it will be bullets.' There was another occasion in one of our night camps on the banks of a tributary of the Amazon. I staggered off to the loo at about two in the morning, and as I walked back towards the camp – and there was jungle all around – I saw these lights approaching, some along the shore towards me, some along the other bank. It was what seemed to be a dozen lamps and lights coming towards us. There was no sound from the camp and no lights from the camp, and I'd heard all these stories about the villages . . . There are awful tales of violent death, people having their throats cut – especially some of the *petroleros*, as they call them, the people who are there to sort of drill for oil. Some of them met some nasty deaths, and I thought, God, they're coming after us. I just dived into my tent and sat there in absolute silence. I turned my torch off, and my heart was thumping. Eventually I looked out through a crack in the curtain and saw about a dozen boats and these people walking up the bank, going up the river, fishing. They go out at night because the fish are easier to catch, and it was just a group of fishermen going by. But for a while it was like the end of *Apocalypse Now*.

So interviewing Michael Palin about his travels isn't the hardest job in the world. You sit there in front of him with a tape recorder and occasionally say, 'Then what happened?' The stories just come tumbling out. John Cleese once said that you'd always know where Michael had been because there'd be a pile of donkey's hind legs.

We were going through the Peruvian jungle, and people like that because it looks uncomfortable. It looks uncomfortable because it is uncomfortable. We were in the jungle but we were OK because we were with this great guide who was looking after us. We were going down some rapids in a river that went through the Amazon into this canyon, and the water was getting quite rough. Our guide, who was an Englishman living in Peru, said, 'I'm so excited! I'm so excited!' and we said, 'You must do this all the time,' and he said, 'No, I've never been here before in my life!' And this was the guide.

At the end, Palin and his band of merry men were stopped from returning to Little Diomede Island by the weather and missed closure of the full circle. 'I felt sad,' he says, 'but not tearful. What the hell, after 50,000 miles of travel, we were one mile out. As the Buddhists would say, only God is perfect.'

Full Circle

'I never call home more than once a week. The point is that you might be looking out over the Pacific, but at home the only thing they're worried about is that the washing machine's leaking or one of the cats has gone missing.'

It was while he was in Borneo, deep in the Sarawak jungle, filming *Full Circle*, that he received the news. 'It was one of the few places of the journey when we were actually out of touch with the rest of the world.' But that's the thing. You go away like Michael Palin goes away and everyone at home worries about you. Where are you going? What will you do if you get sick? Have you packed everything? Got some Imodium? Enough warm clothes? You know it gets cold there at night . . . You're the one in danger. Everyone else, they're staying at home. What's going to happen to them? Surely the worst thing that can go wrong is that maybe it will rain all the time.

When I got back to the coast there was a message from Helen to call home. I felt slightly apprehensive because she didn't usually call unless there was an emergency, but I told myself that she was probably just checking up because I'd been out of contact for three days . . . and that's when Helen told me that they'd found a benign meningioma and were operating within four days.

My instinct was to come back straight away, but Helen was brilliantly controlled and talked me through everything. She said that everything had been arranged, that she would have surgery in four days and that I shouldn't bother rushing back. 'All you'd do is worry. I'd rather you were busy doing something.' It was a very sensible thing to say.

Surveying the beauties of the Atacama Desert in Chile, while filming Full Circle

Helen Palin had suffered from headaches from time to time, as many people do, but while Michael was away she had a terrible migraine. She couldn't sleep and nothing she took made it any better. Her sister said she ought to have a brain scan and so she did. The scan revealed the tumour.

The irony, if you can call it that, was that Michael had just returned from a three-day trip visiting a tribe of head-hunters. John Cleese later famously remarked that he should have brought a spare one back for Helen.

'I didn't have any tears when I heard,' said Palin.

I don't tend to burst into tears at predictable moments. Then, next morning at 6 a.m. I was able to talk to the surgeon. I said, 'What are the dangers? What are the chances that she won't pull through?' Any brain operation sounds terrifying to me, but he reassured me that it was very routine neuro-surgery. The tumour was between the brain and the skull.

Routine or not, it takes a special kind of mental discipline to put something like that out of your head and get on with the job in hand.

Of course you can't forget what's happening if your wife's having an opera-tion of that kind, but if you're working at certain times of the day, you can take your mind off it at least. If I'd been on a plane or waiting at an airport, it would have been intolerable.

No one who saw the fourth episode of *Full Circle* would have suspected a thing.

The feeling that he should be there with her didn't go away and on the day of Helen's operation, when he was in Indonesia, it got too much.

I just thought I should be there with her. What if anything happened? I phoned the hospital and they told me she'd had the operation half an hour earlier and was just coming round. They asked me if I wanted to talk to her. A rather muzzy voice came on the line. Helen sent her love. I was elated. I planned to be home when she came out of hospital. She said I'd be needed then.

And that's how it was: when she was back home, he was there . . . but 'it was a long haul flight and the air in the cabin was dreadful. I ended up with a sore throat and a bad cold. So there was Helen with her head in bandages nursing me. Within two months of the operation, Helen was playing tennis again.'

As for the future? 'I don't feel anxious about leaving her again. You can't con-strain your life and put it on hold because of some hypothetical threat. She hasn't got a progressive disease. The prognosis was right. She's had no problems since the tumour was removed.'

A potentially tragic story with a happy ending – though it did cast Palin's essential middle-classness in a strange light, and there were a number of articles at the time which used cloaked phrases like 'extremes of passion do not fire him'.

Well, there's a certain truth in it. I mistrust extremes unless they can really be carried through. But extremes of passion? No, I don't think it's true to say that – what was the phrase? – 'extremes of passion do not fire him'? I get terribly excited about things, wonderful things . . . the usual things: maybe where I am, a piece of music, a picture I'm looking at, a joke with a friend, a conversation . . . There are days when I'll feel incredibly elated and think this is all very, very wonderful and other days when I feel a bit depressed, but I don't particularly trust either of those extremes because I'm not an extreme person. I resent the idea that I can't feel extremes of passion, or don't get worked up, because I certainly do, but I'm also aware that being extreme in itself doesn't necessarily show that you've got real feelings – it isn't the only way to show that you've got real feelings.

Hemingway's Chair

It's Palin's middle-class reserve that largely accounts for his interest in – or near-obsession with – the writer Ernest Hemingway. Michael Palin, the ever so polite middle-class English public schoolboy and Ernest Hemingway, the personification of the macho man, a man who wrestled bears with his naked hands and fished for giant marlin armed with nothing more than a bottle of bourbon and a dirty glass.

'Yeah, absolutely, he's the antithesis of me. That's what I always liked about Hemingway. He and I are as different as anyone could be.'

Is there a degree of envy there?

There are certain things about Hemingway that I like. First of all, his attraction to foreign places is very much the same as mine, except that he spent longer in places, he really got to know them. He lived in France, he lived in Spain, he lived in Cuba. All the things I wish I could do and I rather admire. I felt that the image of the macho man . . . It's a bit like the nice-man image that I've got. What is underneath it? OK, he was someone who loved shooting animals and catching marlin . . . but he was also someone who believed the art of writing to be so important that he would set pen to paper almost every day.

He might appear aggressive and boorish at times, but he did believe in writing, which is something I also believe in, getting it right, getting it to work. At the same time, he wanted a life. He realized that at the end of the day, you stopped the writing, you have your friends round and you learn about life. And throughout his life he was learning all the time.

I like the idea that he was working at things, learning about things right up to the end of his life. And the other side is that I can see it as an interesting study in someone who was extreme. Hemingway did drink far more than I could ever have done. I'm quite fascinated how someone can do that and still survive. It's just an interesting idea . . .

Of course, Hemingway wasn't the only person in Palin's life to whom those last few sentences might refer.

I mean, dear Graham . . . He would change quite spectacularly when he drank and really, maybe that's why I'm wary of extremes. I love to drink and I love that feeling when you really drink enough to get close to someone and enjoy it, and that's why alcohol can be such a wonderful thing because it's a social thing, whereas pot – and I've nothing against it – is a much more . . . interior thing.

I love drinking with people in a pub, but the idea of drinking to get drunk, getting to that stage where you actually change your personality, does worry me. I was intrigued by Hemingway from that point of view, but also simply because he was very different from me.

In a way, that was what interested me, what you can find out about someone who is the total opposite of yourself. Too many people involve themselves in a very close, tight circle where people only write about a certain number of people. It's like the writers in this country, you know, the Amises and the McEwans. They're great writers, but they all seem terribly, terribly tight. They're always going around with each other, they review each other's books, they talk to each other. As a writer, I think that's really not the way to do it.

You've got to get out there, you know, and Hemingway did that. Went out and explored the world. He hated writers' élites, he hated metropolitan life, he hated writers' awards, all that sort of thing. That wasn't what it was about, that was insidious. The thing you had to do was go out, have experiences, do whatever it was you wanted to do – that was the sort of connection between us, that's why I felt a certain empathy with him in one way. And yet things worked out so differently for him later on . . .

It was Michael Palin who was talking, but it could so easily have been Michael Palin who was the subject of those last paragraphs. He read about Hemingway at school. It's not hard to see how stories of macho achievement would strike a chord with a lad stuck in an institution like Shrewsbury, where the only bell that tolled was the one that told you the tuck shop was open. And it didn't matter how much bigger Palin's world got, he never lost the fascination.

I love *For Whom the Bell Tolls* and *The Old Man and the Sea*. But they're closely followed by a particular favourite of mine, an odd book, very unlike his other books – much more soft and tender, and almost erotic – called *The Garden of Eden*. It was published after his death, almost as if he was trying to keep its existence a secret during his lifetime, for fear that it might not be considered macho. But it's a great book. And his short stories, especially the early Michigan stories, are excellent.

The first inkling of Hemingway in Palin's work came in 1995, with the publication of his first (and so far only) novel, *Hemingway's Chair*. 'Novel writing used to be something of a Python joke, but this time it's serious. Everything comes full circle.' The novel follows quiet post office worker Martin Sproale, who (much like his creator) is a bit of a Hemingway obsessive whose life changes when an American Hemingway scholar comes to town. Like Palin, Sproale is a decent chap, a man who sees the good. But also like Palin, he's got this streak of madness within, a latent non-conformity.

I wanted to really create a character who was the exact opposite of his hero, Ernest Hemingway. Rather than make him a man of action, a bullfighter or fisherman or war reporter, I made him a man of inaction, someone who sits behind a desk in a post office and takes people's money and issues stamps. I wanted him to be doing very much an everyday job. He had to be an ordinary man who, during the course of the story, becomes extraordinary. That's why I chose a relatively humble, but very vital, occupation for him. The book is really written in defence of post offices and workers. If anything, it should become a standard-issue novel for all postal employees.

The title, incidentally, refers to a chair used by Ernest Hemingway on a fishing trip off Peru in 1952 during the filming of *The Old Man and the Sea*.

The story centres on something that's close to Palin's heart – the running down of civic amenities – and *Hemingway's Chair* is based around the feared closure of Sproale's post office.

> There is a real fear that the franchising of the post office will gradually reduce its role in the community to some fully automated system in which you would have no human contact whatsoever. It was this issue of human contact and communication in the face of increasingly sophisticated electronic gadgetry that really interested me.

It was underpinned by Palin's natural warmth and soul and feel for humour.

> A lot of the characters in the book are sort of representative of English society, which in many parts of the country hasn't changed all that much from the Ealing Comedy days – the same prejudices, small-mindedness, deviousness, the same pomposity. It's all good comedy material, and I wanted to make sure there were no dull characters in the book. They each had to have a quirky ingredient that made them special, made them stand out. Which, I've no doubt, was the intention of the Ealing Comedies and of writers such as Kingsley Amis. In fact, the *New York Times* review said it owed more to Kingsley Amis than to John Cleese.

Hemingway's Chair was much more strident than you'd have expected, and in Palin terms it qualified as a polemic, a rant against the growth of mall culture and the homogenization of society.

Palin has always voted Labour, but in 1995 he was quoted as being unhappy with Tony Blair's brand of New Labour and was considering changing his allegiance to the Liberal Democrats. He let it be known that he was a fan of John Prescott: 'He's real fighter and a clear, lucid thinker.' But going over to the other side? Well, it's not really likely.

> I've voted Labour in the last four elections, but to me politics is a bit like sex, it's private. Generally I find the conventional aspects of authority very tiresome. The status quo is something I would always challenge. But I'm very wary of politics itself – it's a very strange profession. I find politicians the most difficult to get on with of all people. They are difficult, defensive, aggressive and false – because they have to be. I really hope it works out for

Palin makes friends with a family of Masai nomads during the Africa leg of
Hemingway's Adventure.

the Labour Party, but there are so many romantic dreams tied up with politics – that one party represents freedom, truth, honesty, and the other one
doesn't. It's bullshit, absolute bullshit. It's an extremely practical business of
how you retain power.

Any approach made by the Labour Party to use his name has been met by a shake
of the head. Like Martin Sproale, Michael Palin's interest in politics is much more
low-level, much more grass-roots. Following his lifelong interest in railways, he's
been high up in the anti-traffic pressure group, Transport 2000, since the mid 1980s,
first as chairman, then in 1990 as president. He has campaigned for stammerers, the
trees at Kenwood House in London (on Hampstead Heath, near where he lives) and
fought to save Camden Parkway cinema (near where he lives). Transport – the under-
investment in the rail system and our over-reliance on cars – has become a bit of
a passion and is one of the few things that gets him worked up in public. 'I'm not
totally against cars, but I believe we have to get the balance right.'

Chapter Nine

The Dark Side of Michael Palin

As we've seen, Palin is an extraordinarily popular man. People who've worked with him love him. People who've met him love him. People who watch his programmes love him. When I was writing this, Roger Mills's words kept coming back, if not exactly to haunt me, then certainly to tease me. 'I don't envy you your job, because in a sense he's as a near perfect a person as you can find and that doesn't necessarily make terribly exciting reading.' Those words are also a bit of a challenge: I *will* make this book exciting. I *will* find the truth behind the façade. I *will* search out the man behind the mask. I *will* unveil the real Michael Palin. There *must* be something . . .

I'd talked to Roger Mills about the sequence at the beginning of *Around the World in Eighty Days* where Michael goes round to various people, asking what they think his chances are of completing the task – insurance brokers, shipping experts, travel people. To a man, they all say he doesn't stand a chance. Ships don't have timetables like they used to, life isn't geared to that sort of travel. The only person who said that Michael would succeed was a bookmaker – and we all know that bookies are never wrong. Anyway, the bookie said, 'I don't think MP would go in for something and not succeed.'

'Well, that actually is a very shrewd point,' said Mills.

Because Michael, for all his niceness, is a winner. He hates losing and you see that . . . On some of these long days and nights on boats when we're away, we play Scrabble, and Michael hates losing. He will try and try and try to the bitter end. I have to say immodestly that I very often beat him. I was a Greek classics student at Oxford. I can put in, for example, obscure words from the Greek that aren't in the dictionary and I think Michael thinks I'm not

---

The dark side of Michael lurks in the undergrowth

playing the game, and he tries and he tries. I think he won the last game we played. He came up with a seven-letter word right at the end and he beat me by something like fifteen. He was triumphant, you could tell.

It's interesting that Roger Mills remembered that Palin won by about fifteen. He must have been some seventy points behind. Odds on, the only way he could have won was to have come up with a seven-letter word. What does that tell us? That he's competitive? That he's lucky? That this is the weakest 'dishing the dirt' attempt you've ever read?

Is Scrabble always the game of choice when you go away?

'Yes, it's popular.'

And do you think that Michael deliberately searches out odd words to use?

Would he search out words to use? I don't know if he consciously does that. He is a writer, so he's an educated person with a very wide vocabulary, but he does come up with some, er, unusual words which I query as well. Ping-pong we play too. He's very competitive. Many a time on trips, Michael has kept the flag flying for us. Doesn't like losing. I'll never forget a tennis match we had in Chile. It went on and on and on in the heat for about three hours because neither of us would lose and it ended up one set each and we were exhausted. Michael, for all that he wears it lightly, doesn't like to lose.

There was one other occasion when it seemed that Michael's competitive nature got the better of him. In 1984, when he was filming *Palin's Column*, a short series where he went to the Isle of Wight and wrote four newspaper columns for the *Isle of Wight County Press*, he was accused of falsely enhancing his conker during the Isle of Wight Conker championships. Fed it steroids or something.

It was pickled for me by a firm of conker consultants. I'd rather not say exactly what they did, but no illegal substances or steroids were used, though I believe vinegar may have been applied. It might even have been lightly baked.

When the series finished, Palin explained, 'The great conker débâcle was a set-up invented by the production team to pep up the series.'

So there you have it. The Dark Side of Michael Palin. He doesn't like to lose – even when he's playing conkers.

Michael contemplates his dark side over a bar of chocolate

Chapter Ten

The Last of the Big Journeys – Part 2

'Coming home after months and months is one of the hardest things to do.'
But there must be compensations to coming home?

> When you're away, there are certain days when you dream about being in
> your own bed surrounded by your own things. My favourite fantasy is open-
> ing my own fridge door and seeing bits of food that have been there for three
> days and thinking, 'That's ours,' and knowing you don't have to search for
> a restaurant. Things like brown bread, hard English cheese, white wine, mak-
> ing my own coffee, seem all the better for having been away.

Travel was getting harder and after finishing *Full Circle*, Michael Palin said to himself, 'Well, I know I'll always want to travel, but this is going to be the last of the big
journeys that we do.'

Hemingway's Chair wasn't the end of Palin's fascination with Ernest Hemingway,
though, and in 1999 he made a series that combined his love of travel with his
Hemingway fixation – *Michael Palin's Hemingway Adventure*. The point was made at
the time that it was a man famous for putting two chips up his nose (in *A Fish Called
Wanda*) retracing the footsteps of a man who ended his life with a double-barrel shot-
gun in his mouth. A four-part series (a mini-jaunt in Palin's terms), it saw him doing
what was, by now, expected: getting his passport out and going around the world. Bar-
hopping in Cuba, marlin-fishing in Florida, running with the bulls in Pamplona (well,
watching people running with the bulls), rounding up cattle in Montana, hanging out
in Venice during a masked ball . . . Like everything he does, it had 'quality' stamped
all over, and yet *Michael Palin's Hemingway Adventure* was criticized.

Preparing for another adventure – travelling light not an option

It's difficult to know why it caused such ire. Certainly, there was nothing wrong with the programme. It was sumptuously made, gorgeous to watch and painstakingly put together. Maybe it was that people were fed up with 'that nice Michael Palin'. Most probably, it was simply the wrong programme at the wrong time.

Criticism is something that Palin lives with and, to be fair, he's a lot more accepting of it than many stars of his stature. But just as the one thing he can't abide in his team is incompetence, the one thing he can't stand in critics is what he considers laziness. One review of *Pole to Pole* in the *Observer* said that it 'made him want to sleep and never wake up'. That impressed Michael. 'Well, fuck you, I thought. All the effort we've put in, yet you won't put the effort into a proper review.'

It's easy to be jealous. These programmes don't look like work. When I asked Roger Mills if his was the best job in television, he said, 'Yes, it is a fantastic job. My job's a fantastic job, but Michael's is a superbly fantastic job.'

There was a story Michael told me that, coming from almost anyone else, would have sounded at best naïve, at worst simply stupid. Instead, it sounded hurt, like a schoolboy who'd been betrayed by someone he thought was his mate.

I was doing *Weekend*, the play, and was asked to do an interview for the *Sunday Times* magazine and, of course, the producers were very happy about that. And that's another thing. Very often one does publicity because the people involved in making the programme, in putting the play on, in making the film, have all worked very hard, and you're the one who can make their work get noticed, so you have a responsibility to them and their work.

I agreed to do this interview. We were rehearsing the play in Chelsea, so I suggested somewhere nearby, and, you know, the *Sunday Times* were paying and she said let's have a nice meal. So I suggested Bibendum and we went there and had a very nice meal and a good talk, and when the piece came out it was really very snide and said things like, 'Michael Palin took me to a restaurant where the waiters all know him.' I mean, most of the restaurants I go to know who I am and the last thing I'm going to do is take some *Sunday Times* journalist somewhere to show off that I'm known. The whole piece was pretty unpleasant and was saying, 'Michael Palin's pretty shallow, he hasn't got much to say . . . He's hiding a lot, he's someone who doesn't like to talk about himself.' Anyway, the long and short of it was that it came out, fair enough. Someone said later that this journalist was chosen because she will say what she wants to say and she was sent out to get the nice Michael Palin, to find the reality behind the mask. And I thought, well, what a silly game.

That surprises you?

Yeah, well. There are certain things, certain experiences that educate you. That one because . . . we actually got on very well and I enjoyed talking to her, that's why I was very surprised at the end of it, and surprised too that a journalist should be given orders like that and should be prepared to carry them out in that clumsy way. Since then, I've avoided 'thought' pieces on Michael Palin, because I don't really think they get anywhere. If someone wants to talk about my work, I'll talk about the work. I think that's very interesting, because actually you find out why you did what you did. People make observations which make you look closely at what you do. But if I want psychoanalysis, I'll go and see a psychoanalyst.

'He does get hurt by adverse criticism,' said Mills.

He was very stunned when what he considered to be his papers turned on him and they were venomous about the Hemingway series. What hurt Michael was that they were personal. They were personal attacks on him, and that certainly stung. When it becomes venomous and personal, logic goes out of the window.

'Every now and then, obviously, there are some people bursting with a sort of bilious resentment at the fact that I am still employed for doing things that are largely quite popular,' says Palin.

> Occasionally that sort of gushes out, but with the *Hemingway's Adventure* actually there were a few really awful reviews. I mean, beyond just saying we don't think this is a good idea. The balance was wrong, beyond constructive. It was just abuse, and mostly from the papers I read, like the *Guardian* and the *Independent*. There's a real bile there which slightly frightened me.
>
> What happens is, I think, the programme is known as *Michael Palin's Adventure*, which, of course, is what the title is. But I mean, you expect certain critics to look beneath that and talk about how the programme is put together and all that. And, in fact, the crew and the technical side of it are terribly important to me. As far as I am concerned, I always think if you are a television reviewer you should know those sorts of facts and, of course, that was never noticed at all. Nigel's camera work was usually alluded to at some point. But Nigel's won BAFTA awards for best camera work for what he's done with me. John Prichard won best sound with the Hemingway series. You know, no one ever mentioned them in their column. And I think this is where some critics are lacking, especially critics with more of an intellectual leaning. But they all seem to fall for the Michael Palin image, which must be irritating for people to read about. It irritates me when people say there's that nice Michael Palin who can do no wrong.

If those technical people weren't there, I'm sure everyone would notice immediately, but you must accept that it's got to be *Michael Palin's Hemingway Adventure*, because if they didn't have that 'Michael Palin' there . . . who's going to watch *Hemingway's Adventure*?

> Yes, I'm aware of that. It's not the title, it's more the way it's approached after that. A good critic would see that it's called what it's called to get the viewers. But let's look at some of the other things. I mean, I don't think the director was ever once mentioned in the Hemingway reviews. He and I put the whole thing together really – and the producer – I mean, that wasn't mentioned.

That's the drawback to working with someone as famous as you.

> Well, this is what this sort of fame is. You know, it's celebrity certainly in that people tend to know me where I go and they're very friendly and jolly on the

whole. But it gets in the way at other times and sometimes it seems that some people think I just stand in front of a cheetah with a white backdrop . . .

We could say that it demonstrates his love of travel, and no doubt that comes into it to a large extent. But also Palin's competitive nature, and his restlessness, would have meant that he would not only go off on another trip but make it to one of the toughest places on earth – the Sahara – travelling through some of the most inhospitable countries in the world.

'It's probably one of the most demanding places we've been to,' admitted Roger Mills.

Is that why they're going?

'No, it came about because we were talking and I said, "Why don't we go to the old French empire? No one's ever done that on television," and Michael refined that to the Sahara, which is a more attractive concept.'

It wasn't a deliberate ploy? A riposte to those critics who said he's getting soft?

'I think there might be an element of that, yes.'

That competitive thing?

I think so, yes. We could have chosen to do some of this comfortably. We could have gone up the Niger in a customized boat and hired cooks and nice comfortable beds and things like that. But we've deliberately chosen to go the way the ordinary people would have to go – on an old riverboat which is, as they say, a truly African experience.

Mills is cautiously blasé about the dangers. These are countries where political instability is a way of life, where being a cowboy or a pirate is a legitimate career option. It's dangerous, but it's also great telly. Did they travel under the invisible wing of the British authorities? Did they work in conjunction with the security forces at all?

No, I don't want to get too close to these people. We tell them when we're going to be there, but if we run into any cowboys, I'm not sure what they can do. We've got a satellite phone and if there was time to get a satellite phone out, I'd call the production office rather than the British Embassy. But we've had experts on security coming in and saying crazy things. We had one the other day who said, 'If you find yourself in a minefield you didn't realize you were in – and remember, there's a lot of minefields where you're going – stand still, don't move. If necessary, stay there for four days while we get help to you.' Totally crazy things like that. They play on your nerves, but once you get there, of course, it's just different.

Epilogue

The thing about Michael is that at the end of one of these series, he always says never again. 'That's it. It was so awful I'm never going to do anything like that again.' Of course he always does, always has, probably always will. We always say, give him nine months and he'll come round.
ROGER MILLS

For a forty-seven-year-old, Palin's very fit, and considering he's actually fifty-seven, he's not doing bad. He runs three or four miles three times a week, eats properly and looks after himself. He's got a serious 'good restaurant' habit and loves to wine and dine, but he's somehow got the balance right. He's one of those people who radiates good health – the smart but casual clothes he favours (denim and stuff that looks relaxed but is actually probably quite expensive) hang off him and he looks comfortable rather than elegant. It helps too that he's kept his hair, and it hasn't gone grey.

'It's getting harder for Michael. He's a very fit man, but if you look at him, of course, there's a bit of wear and tear there. But he's fit, he still runs regularly because he knows that health is the bedrock of everything he does,' says Mills.

So he's healthy, but you can't help but think the Sahara programme will be the last. By the time it goes out (scheduled for autumn 2002) he'll be fifty-nine. By the time they'd get round to another one, he'd be at least sixty-one, and you'd have to wonder why he still does it. Clem Vallance has retired. If the ratings for *Sahara* are lowish, like they were for *Hemingway's Adventure* . . .

So what's next? Looking back at Palin's career, it seems marked by decisions that are relatively brave.

Brave or foolhardy. Whatever it is, I just do things because they feel right to me. I think that's something that's come from *Python*; it gave me a confidence that if you really believe in something and in the way it should be done, and you stick with those beliefs, then you're going to produce something better than if you wait for someone to tell you what you should be doing.

What about doing this properly? Writing his own story, an autobiography? He's a serious writer and has kept diaries since *Python* started.

> I think there's something interesting about personal experience, but you don't have to call it 'the autobiography'. I've often thought about putting together a biography of the *Python* years from my diaries, but I'd probably get sued by the others . . .

'It'll be very interesting to see where Michael goes. There'll come a time when physically he'll have to stop,' said Roger Mills.

> But what will he do? He can act, he can write, he can present . . . I don't know what he'll do. Probably he'll find another string to his bow. The only thing you can be sure of is that he'll never sit back on his laurels and enjoy his well-earned wealth.

The work ethic. It's a blessing and a curse. Even now, when he's nowhere near the final furlong of his career, he can look back at a body of work that, in its scope and scale, is really second to none. Most people would probably be happy to take their foot off the accelerator, but Palin seems curiously reluctant to do that. Reluctant or unable.

More travel? Is the thrill still there?

> Oh yes, I still get an excitement, a buzz, from being somewhere different. I love going to different places, with different languages, different climates, and not knowing what I am going to find there. It's that odd feeling of facing up to something that I've never encountered before. I feel as though it is as close to changing your life utterly as you can get while still remaining the same. But I suppose that's why I became an actor. I am interested in putting myself in another situations. To me, travelling is part of drama; it is a very dramatic thing – the people you meet, the things that are new. It's refreshing and revitalizing and exciting.

Michael Palin's in an enviable position. He can do what he likes, go where he wants and presumably he's at a stage with the BBC when he could pretty much come up with whatever he likes.

There's still push and pull a little bit. I mean, the Sahara journey, I would have liked to have done a series of seven programmes about that, maybe fifty minutes or forty-five minutes each. The BBC are very much against that – for whatever reason I can never quite fathom. They want to do shorter blocks and a longer programme. Like four one-hour programmes. But my relationship with the BBC is friendly, we talk.

Actually I'd love to do a programme about religions. That is the one thing that does get me closest to a sort of political view at the moment, the way that we still have a streak of racism and bigotry in this country. I think that's the most unpleasant thing about England. The worst thing about it is that it's not a real thing, it just comes from ignorance. It comes from fear, it comes from a feeling of being under siege. I'd love to do something which says, look, the plurality of what's happening in this country is one of our greatest strengths. We have a mountain of different people with different religions from different parts of the world in this country, and I think this is really one of the strongest and most hopeful things for our future. We've got to get it right. The idea of this country being swamped by people and by different religions . . . we've got to deal with this. We've always had people coming in from abroad and we've always welcomed them. That's been our strength. Just because someone is a Muslim, it doesn't mean their religion is not as good as yours. Very often you can look at different religions and say, well, actually that's *better*. I'd love to do something like that. Not a heavy thing, but just something to enlighten people about other countries and other religions.

It's an interesting idea. Michael Palin becoming a political figure. Well, not really a political figure, but someone who deals in political subjects, who can use their skills to do something a little more than get good ratings. More and more, it seems that Palin's real gift is in communication. We can talk about the writing, the acting, the books, the films, the telly . . . but what links everything together is his ability to communicate, to make it interesting and to make people want to listen. 'There's a huge amount I'd like to do. I'm quite interested in art at the moment. And I'd love to learn more about that.'

Art is Palin's secret passion and, like a lot of wealthy people who'd rather not make a big fuss about their wealth, he's started to bring his passion to life, becoming a bit of a collector. He's also put his passion on the small screen, and has made a couple of programmes about art and artists who are close to his heart. The first one he did was on the Scottish artist Anne Redpath.

The reason we did that was because I had a couple of her paintings and someone from BBC Scotland wanted to do a programme and find some celebrities who owned her work. My name came up, so they approached me.

In the end, the programme was about one of the paintings that hangs in the Palins' dining-room. 'She painted it around 1948 and I've always wondered whether that view was still there, so we went to France, where she lived, and made a programme about me going back there and trying to find it.' Of course they found it. 'It was very much the same, in fact. And we actually ate in a café which is a little building with railings, just the same as in the painting that I look at when I'm at home.'

Working on the Anne Redpath programme was right up Palin's street – and probably gives a clue as to what he'll do in the future – working on something he's very interested in, with a small team all interested in the subject . . . and if possible away from London.

I went to a Turner exhibition the other day. He's a great man. His ability to record the detail of a scene must have been extraordinary. I asked someone there, an expert, and he said Turner kept a lot of notes and would make a little quick sketch, but a lot of it was just from having a fantastic memory. If you look at Turner's paintings, there's nothing wishy-washy about them, nothing indeterminate. He's in there, bang! The rocks, trees, perspective, the waterfall, figures on the right, figures on the left. Either he had this fantastic memory or he was a terrific storyteller. Natural dramatist.

I'd love to write a little film about one of Turner's expeditions, because he went off to Europe with his friends and did his thing, that was his job. A bit like what I do, in a way. You're going to somewhere rather beautiful and you've got to bring back the material because, my God, that's your living. I'd love to do something like that . . . You know, what did they talk about in the evenings? Politics? It was quite an exciting time then. It was a fighting time, the end of the Napoleonic wars, a time of parliamentary reforms . . . And these characters physically and spiritually went off and explored . . .

You know what it's like when you're talking to someone and suddenly they're off somewhere else, having a conversation with themselves?

. . . And really bring something back . . . Someone came up to me when I was at that exhibition and said, 'Doesn't that make you want to be there?'

Index

Figures in *italics* indicate illustrations.

Alachouzos, John 15, 16
Allen, Benedict 130
American Friends 100, 122, *122*, 123–4
Amis, Kingsley 142
*And Now for Something Completely
    Different* 67, 68
Around the World in Eighty Days 11, 20,
    110–11, 112, *113*, 114–17, 119–21,
    122, 124, 125, 126, 129, 133, 145
'Astrology Sketch' 53
At Last The 1948 Show 44, 47
Attenborough, Sir David 57, 130

'Barber' sketch 55
Barclay, Humphrey 44, 45, 56, 57
Barker, Ronnie 43
Bates, Simon 119
BBC 18, 25, 37, 39, 45, 47, 49, 56, 57,
    58, 64, 66, 72, 77, 89–92, 95, 104,
    111, 112, 114, 117, 121, 122, 126,
    130, 156–7
Beatles 41, 51, 56, 61
Bennett, Alan 19, 97, 98–9
Bert Fegg's Nasty Book for Boys and Girls
    89
Beyond the Fringe 36
Birkdale prep school 28
Blair, Tony 24, 142
Bleasdale, Alan 19, 93, 102, 122
Bonzo Dog Doo Dah Band 44
Booth, Connie 51
Boothroyd, Basil 31
Braden, Bernard 32
Braden, Chris 32
Brasenose College, Oxford 30–31, 38
Brazil 89, 93, 94, 99–100, *100*
Broadcasting Standards Council 116
Brooke-Taylor, Tim 43, 44
Buñuel, Luis: *Discreet Charm of the
    Bourgeoisie* 81

Cambridge Footlights 31, 39, 43, 44, 111
Cambridge Review 41
Cambridge University 27, 30, 31, 35, 39, 51
Camden Parkway cinema, London 143
Chapman, Graham 9, *10*, 13, 35, 39, 40,
    40, 41, 44, 45, 47, 48, 50–55, 62–6,
    68, 69, 71, 74, 75, 76, *76*, 79, 86, 87,
    87, 89, 110, 140

Charisma Records 69
'Cheese Shop, The' (sketch) 62
Chrysalis Records 69
Clare College, Cambridge 29
Cleese, John 9, *10*, 12, 13, 19, 35, 39–40,
    40, 41, 43, 44, 45, 47–52, 54, *54*, 55,
    58, 61–7, 69, 71, 74–7, 80, 83, 85, 86,
    89, 102, *103*, 104, 105, 112, 135, 136,
    138, 142
Cleveland, Carol 13, 56
Coffey, Denise *34*, 36, 44
Collieu, Eric 30
*Complete and Utter History of the
    World, A* 45, 69
Connery, Sean 93
Cook, Peter 36, 67, 90
Corbett, Ronnie 43
Cotton, Bill, Jr 57
Cotton, Billy 39
Crichton, Charles 102
Cryer, Barry 43
Curry, Tim *90*
Curtis, Jamie Lee 102, *103*, 105
'Cycling Tour, The' 63, 90
Cyril and the Dinner Party 94
Cyril and the House of Commons 94

Dalí, Salvador 50
De Niro, Robert 9, 93, 100
'Dead Parrot' sketch 53, 54–5, *54*
Dibley, Gwen 48
Do Not Adjust Your Set (DNAYS) 38, 39,
    44, 45, 49, 50
Dodd, Ken 39, 84
Dress, The 93
'Dull Life of a City Stockbroker, The' 53
Duvall, Shelley 93

Ealing Comedies 142
East of Ipswich 93, 100–101, *101*, 102,
    123
Edgar Allen & Co 27
Edinburgh Festival 32, 41
Edmonds, Noel 111, 114
Elliott, Denholm 9, 91, 93, 97, *97*
Eton College 101

Fawlty Towers 49, 51, 65, 89, 102
Feldman, Marty 35, 41, *42*, 43, 44, 52, 53

Fiennes, Ranulph 130
Fierce Creatures 104–5, *105*, 124, 135
Fish Called Wanda, A 10, 19, 86, 93, 102,
    103, 104, 105, 114, 129, 149
'Fish Slapping Dance' 93
Frears, Stephen 89
Friendly, Fred 56
Frost, David 9, 18, 43, 44, 45
Frost Report, The 35, 43–4, 47
Frost Show, The 36
Full Circle 11, 17, 105, 116, 133–8, 149
Funny Game 89

GBH 93, 102, 106, 122, *125*
Gilliam, Terry 9, *10*, 12–13, 39, 40, 45,
    47, 49–50, 52, 58, 62, 65, *65*, 66, 67,
    69, 71, 74, 85, 86, 89, 94, *95*, 99,
    100, 115
Goldstone, John 72
Goodies, The 84
Goon Show, The 28, 31, 59, 67
Gospel Oak, north London 22, 25, 70
Great Railway Journeys of the World 111,
    114
Greene, Graham 29
'Gumby, D.P.' 55

Handmade Films 72, 99, 111
Harrison, George 72, 75, 89, 94–5, 99
Have I Got News For You 21
Hemingway, Ernest 25, 122, 139–42,
    149
Hemingway's Chair (Palin) 141–2, 149
Hewison, Robert 30, 31–2, 39, 40, 92,
    107, 111
Hollywood Bowl 33, 78–9
Hordern, Michael 93
How to Irritate People 45, 54, 55
Howard, Trevor 93, 97
Howard Davies, John 48–9, 57
Hughes, Terry 89

Idle, Eric 9, *10*, *34*, 36, 39, 40, 41, 43, 44,
    48, 50–53, 56, 63, 64, 67, 68, 69, 71,
    72, 74, 83, 86, 87, 89, 95, 112, 123,
    134
I'm Sorry, I'll Read That Again 41, 44
Island Records 69

Jabberwocky 94, 95
Jack and the Beanstalk 122
Jagger, Mick 79
Jason, David 34, 36, 44
Jay, Anthony 43
Jerome, Jerome K. 89
Jethro Tull 69
John, Elton 65
Jones, Terry 9, *10*, 13, 32, *33*, *34*, 35, 36,
   36, 39, 40, *40*, 41, 43, 44, 45, 48–53,
   55, 56, 62–9, 71, 76, 81, 83, 86, 89–92,
   95, *95*, 104, 107, 109, 111, 114

Keaton, Buster 48
Kenwood House, Hampstead 143
Kington, Miles 114
Kline, Kevin 102, *103*, 105
Kurtzman, Harvey 49–50

Labour Party 24, 142, 143
Law, John 57
Lawson, Mark 121
Lean, David 48
Led Zeppelin 69
Lennon, John 41, 51
Lewis, Martyn: *Success* 18
Liberal Democrats 142
Life of Brian 15, 72–8, 83, 93, 104
Limerick Book, The 94
'Loitering Within Tent' 32
London Weekend Television (LWT) 37
Lowell, Carey 135

McCartney, Paul 41, 51, 55, 56
MacDonald, Aimi 44, 47
MacNaughton, Ian 48
Mad magazine 49
Magdalen College, Oxford 31
Meakin, Nigel 152
Meaning of Life, The 6, 81, *81*, 82, 83,
   92, 93, 95
Michael Palin Centre for Stammering
   Children, London 22, 104
Michael Palin's Hemingway's Adventure
   11, 19, *143*, 149–52, 155
Milchan, Arnon 100
Miller, Jonathan 111
Milligan Preserved (recording) 31
Milligan, Spike 31, 47–50, 67, 75
Mills, Michael 45
Mills, Roger 11, 16–18, 86, 111–12, 114,
   117, 119, 126, 127–8, 133, 145–6, 150,
   151, 153, 155, 156
Mirrorstone, The 94
Missionary, The 6, 7, 15–16, 93, 95–6, 95,
   96
Monday Night at Home 31
Montreux Golden Rose award 43
Monty Python and the Holy Grail 60,
   67–71, *70*, 72, 74, 75, 83, 86, 87, 134
*Monty Python Live at the Hollywood
   Bowl* 89
Monty Python's Flying Circus 9, 21, 35,
   41, 44, 45–60, 61–7, 72

Moore, Dudley 67
Moore, Stephen *91*
Morecambe, Eric 57
Mowbray, Malcolm 97
Muggeridge, Malcolm 77
Muir, Frank 43

Nicholson, Jack 79
Norden, Dennis 43
Not the Nine o'Clock News 86
Now! (pop music show) 38
Number 27 93, 101, 123

O'Brien, Denis 72, 99, 111
Occidental College, California 39
Oddie, Bill 43
'Oscar Wilde' sketch 63
Oxford Revue 41
Oxford Revue Group 32
Oxford Theatre Group 32
Oxford Union Cellars 31
Oxford University 18, 25, 29–32, 35, 38,
   39, 51, 107, 114, 115, 123

Palin, Angela (Michael's sister) 25, 27, 28,
   123
Palin, Brita (Michael's great-grandmother)
   123
Palin, Reverend Edward (Michael's great-
   grandfather) 123
Palin, Helen (née Gibbins; Michael's wife)
   22, *23*, 25, 29, 101, 137–9
Palin, Mary (Michael's mother) 27, 28
Palin, Rachel (Michael's daughter) *24*, 25,
   31
Palin, Ted (Michael's father) 27–8, 29, 59,
   104, 109
Palin, Tom (Michael's elder son) *24*, 25,
   61
Palin, William (Michael's younger son) *24*,
   25, 31
Palin's Column 117, *118*, 146
Palmer, Tony 39, 48
Patel, Mash 22
Peel, John 28–9
Pethig, Hazel 9
Pink Floyd 69
Pole to Pole 11, 124–9, 133, 150
Powell, Tristan 123
Prescott, John 142
Presley, Elvis 59
Prichard, John 152
Private Function, A 19, 93, 97–9, *98*
Puttnam, David 101
Python stage show 32

Q series 67
Q5 48, 49

Ranmoor, Sheffield 27
Ravenscroft, John (John Peel) 28–9
Rediffusion 37
Redpath, Anne 157–8
Reform Club, London 119

Reptile Protection Trust 116
Ripping Yarns 90–92, 95
Rolling Stones 79
Russell, Ken 39
Rutland Weekend Television 89

Sahara 153, 155, 157
St John's College, Oxford 123
Saturday Night, Sunday Morning 77
Saturday Night Live 78, 80
Scott, Captain Robert 130
Secrets 89
Seedy Entertainers 31
Sheringham, Norfolk 28
Shrewsbury public school 28–9, 31, 141
'Slapstick Sequence' 32, *33*
Small Harry and the Toothache Pills 94
Smith, Maggie 9, 93, 96, 97, *98*, 99
Southwold, Suffolk 25, 28, 29, 101
Souza, John Philip: 'The Liberty Bell
   March' 58
'Spanish Inquisition, The' (sketch) 56
Speight, Johnny 57
Stockwood, Mervyn, Bishop of Southwark
   77
Stoppard, Tom 89
Stuart-Harris, Graham 28
Stuart-Harris family 28
Sunday Times 150
Sykes, Eric 57

Take It from Here 31
Thames Television 35, 37, 45
That Was the Week that Was 57
Three Men in a Boat 89, 91
Time Bandits 93, 93
Took, Barry 35, 43, 45, 84
Transport 2000 143
Turner, J. M.W. 158
Two Ronnies, The 39, 84

US Comedy Arts Festival, Aspen 87

Vallance, Clem 111–12, 125, 133, 155

Waterhouse, Keith 43
Weekend 150
Weldon, Huw 57
Whicker, Alan 112, 115, 120
White, Michael 69
Whitehouse, Mary 63–4
Whitley, Edward 15, 16
Wilcox, Desmond 57
Wood, Duncan 64
Wood, Michael 130
Worcester College, Oxford 29–30
Wordsworth, William 30

Young Ones, The 86

Zeffirelli, Franco 73